CRAFTING SCALABLE AND RESILIENT BUSINESS MODELS FOR LONG-TERM SUCCESS

Fidelia Agwuncha

Copyright © 2022. All rights reserved.

Crafting Scalable and Resilient Business Models for Long-Term Success

Fidelia Agwuncha

No part of this book may be reproduced or transmitted in any form or by any means, electronic or mechanical, including photocopying, recording, or by any information storage and retrieval system, without permission in writing from the Copyright owner.

Any information is to be used for educational and information purposes only. It should never be substituted for financial advice.

The author or publisher does not in any way endorse any commercial products or services linked from other websites to this book.

Globally Available

ISBN 978-5-3793-8090-8

Published in Nigeria in 2022
Emphaloz Publishing House

A catalogue record of this book will be available from the National Library of Nigeria.

TABLE OF CONTENT

Table Of Content iii
Foreword iv
Introduction vi

CHAPTER ONE
FUNDAMENTALS OF BUILDING SCALABLE BUSINESS MODELS 1

CHAPTER TWO
LEAN STRATEGIES FOR SUSTAINABLE BUSINESS GROWTH 15

CHAPTER THREE
DEVELOPING RESILIENT BUSSINESS MODELS IN UNCERTAIN MARKET 59

CHAPTER FOUR
LEVERAGING DATA ANALYTICS FOR LONG TERM SUCCESS 77

CHAPTER FIVE
FINANCIAL PLANNING FOR SCALABLE AND RESILIENT BUSINESS 91

CHAPTER SIX
INNOVATION AS A CORE DRIVER OF BUSINESS SUSTAINABILITY 109

CHAPTER SEVEN
BUILDING AGILE TEAMS TO SUPPORT SCALABE MODEL 131

CHAPTER EIGHT
TECHNOLOGY INTEGRATION FOR OPERATIONAL EFFICIENCY 139

Foreword

In the world of business, scalability is the ultimate measure of success. It separates companies that experience short-term growth from those that thrive in the long term, navigating market fluctuations, rising customer demands, and the ever-changing landscape of technology. In **CRAFTING SCALABLE AND RESILIENT BUSINESS MODELS FOR LONG TERM SUCCESS**, we delve into one of the most critical concepts of modern entrepreneurship: how to build and sustain a business that not only grows but grows efficiently and profitably.

This book explores the building blocks of scalability, from developing a value proposition that resonates across diverse markets to creating a revenue model that drives exponential growth without proportionally increasing costs. It provides readers with the practical tools to structure operations in a way that harnesses technology, reduces inefficiencies, and capitalizes on economies of scale. In today's business environment, where competition is fierce, and innovation is paramount, this knowledge is indispensable.

Entrepreneurs, business leaders, and investors alike will find in these pages a comprehensive roadmap for navigating the challenges of expansion. Each chapter addresses key components of scalable success from operational efficiency and customer acquisition to adaptability and risk management. By understanding and applying these principles, businesses can set themselves on a path to sustainable growth, market competitiveness, and long-term success.

In this era of rapid change, agility and scalability are not just desirable, they are essential. The insights in this book offer a framework for leaders who aim to position their businesses for future growth while maintaining profitability, efficiency, and flexibility. The lessons within are timeless, and their impact can be transformative.

INTRODUCTION

The modern business environment is one of constant change, where innovation and rapid adaptability are not just advantages, but necessities. Within this context, building a business model that can scale, growing in size, revenue, and reach without a proportional increase in costs is an essential component of long-term success. Many businesses can thrive in their early stages, but the real challenge arises when they try to expand while maintaining efficiency, profitability, and market competitiveness.

Scalability is more than a buzzword; it is the cornerstone of sustainable business growth. A scalable business model ensures that as demand increases, operational systems can adapt, resources are optimally allocated, and profitability remains intact or even improves. It is a concept that touches every part of a business, from the product or service offering to the revenue model, customer acquisition strategies, and internal processes.

The purpose of this book is to provide a comprehensive exploration of the core principles, strategies, and components that drive scalable business models. Through these insights, entrepreneurs, business leaders, and investors alike can gain a deeper understanding of what it takes to scale their businesses effectively. The goal is to create models that not only work in the short term but are designed to endure and grow in the face of evolving markets, technological advances, and changing customer needs.

This book begins with an overview of scalability itself, defining what it means and why it is crucial to business success. From there, we will delve into the various components that contribute to scalability, such as crafting a compelling value proposition, developing a flexible and profitable revenue model, ensuring operational efficiency, and mastering customer acquisition and retention. Along the way, we will explore real-world examples of companies that have successfully scaled their operations and the strategies they used to achieve this.

Whether you are launching a startup, seeking to expand an established business, or looking to invest in high-potential ventures, this book offers practical insights and strategic frameworks that will guide you in building a scalable business model that can thrive in any market condition. The path to scalability is challenging but achievable with the right knowledge and approach. Let's embark on this journey to understand the fundamentals of building scalable businesses that are not only profitable today but can adapt and grow sustainably into the future.

CHAPTER ONE

FUNDAMENTALS OF BUILDING SCALABLE BUSINESS MODELS

In today's dynamic and rapidly evolving business landscape, scalability has become one of the most critical factors for long-term success. A scalable business model ensures that an organization can grow and expand without being constrained by limited resources or inefficiencies. While building a business model that works in the short term is relatively straightforward, creating one that is scalable and sustainable over time requires a deeper understanding of various business principles, strategic foresight, and a relentless focus on innovation.

What is Scalability in Business?

Scalability in business refers to the ability of a company to increase its output or revenue without a corresponding increase in costs or resources. In a scalable business model, the growth in sales, customers, or product demand does not lead to a proportional rise in expenses or operational complexity. This means that a company can grow and serve more customers or expand into new markets while maintaining or even improving profitability.

Importance of scalability

Scalability is crucial for the long-term success and growth of any business. It allows a company to expand without being constrained by limitations in resources, costs, or operational complexity. Here are the key reasons why scalability is important:

a. Sustainable Growth

Scalability ensures that a business can grow without increasing operational costs in proportion to its growth. This allows a company to handle more customers, transactions, or sales without losing efficiency or profitability, which supports sustainable and healthy expansion.

b. Increased Profit Margins

As businesses scale, they benefit from economies of scale—producing more with lower per-unit costs. This often results in higher profit margins since revenue grows faster than costs. The ability to maintain or increase profitability as the business grows is a major advantage of scalability.

c. Operational Efficiency

Scalable models encourage businesses to streamline processes and adopt technologies that enable greater efficiency. Automation, cloud computing, and data-driven strategies help companies handle larger volumes of work with fewer resources, making it easier to scale operations while maintaining quality.

d. Market Competitiveness

Scalability allows businesses to quickly respond to changes in demand and market opportunities, giving them a competitive edge. Companies that can scale rapidly are better positioned to capture market share, expand into new regions, and capitalize on emerging trends.

e. Attraction to Investors

Scalable business models are highly attractive to investors because they indicate the potential for rapid growth without proportional increases in costs. Businesses that demonstrate scalability often have higher valuations and greater access to funding, which fuels further expansion.

f. Adaptability to Market Fluctuations

A scalable business can more easily adapt to changing market conditions, such as fluctuations in demand or shifts in customer preferences. By having a flexible and scalable infrastructure, businesses can pivot or adjust strategies without compromising their operations or profitability.

g. Enhanced Customer Experience

Scalable businesses are able to maintain or improve the quality of their products or services as they grow. By investing in scalable systems and processes, companies can ensure that they continue to meet customer expectations, regardless of size or market reach.

h. Global Expansion

A scalable business model makes it easier to enter new markets and expand globally. With scalable infrastructure and systems, companies can replicate their operations across different regions, offering their products or services to a larger audience without the complexity of starting from scratch in each market.

i. Risk Mitigation

Scalability helps businesses build a foundation that can handle larger volumes of transactions and potential challenges, reducing the risk of operational bottlenecks or breakdowns as they grow. This resilience is essential for companies aiming for long-term success in a volatile business environment.

j. Long-Term Success

Ultimately, scalability is key to ensuring that a business can grow in a sustainable, efficient, and profitable manner. It lays the groundwork for long-term success by preparing a business to handle increased demand, adapt to changes, and continually innovate while maintaining cost control and quality.

A scalable business model typically has the following characteristics:

Low Incremental Costs: As the business grows, the cost of acquiring new customers or producing additional products remains low.

Efficient Use of Technology: Scalable businesses often rely on technology to automate processes, reduce human intervention, and manage larger volumes of activity.

Flexibility and Adaptability: A scalable business model is flexible enough to adapt to changing market conditions and customer needs without disrupting operations.

Sustainable Growth Strategies: Growth is supported by sustainable business practices that prevent overextension or operational strain.

Understanding scalability is essential for entrepreneurs, business leaders, and investors as it determines how well a company can handle growth and respond to opportunities in the marketplace.

Key Components of a Scalable Business Model

Several key components contribute to the scalability of a business model. By focusing on these elements, businesses can create a solid foundation for sustainable and profitable growth.

a. Value Proposition

At the heart of any scalable business model is a strong value proposition. A value proposition articulates the unique benefits that a company offers to its customers and how it solves their problems better than its competitors. It is critical for a business to define its value proposition clearly because it drives demand, customer loyalty, and market positioning.

A scalable value proposition is one that appeals to a broad market, can be easily communicated, and is compelling enough to drive customer acquisition. It should also be adaptable to different customer segments or geographic regions as the company expands.

For example, companies like Uber and Airbnb built their value propositions around convenience, cost-effectiveness, and accessibility, which allowed them to scale quickly across multiple markets.

b. Revenue Model

A revenue model outlines how a company generates income. To build a scalable business, the revenue model must support growth without relying on linear expansion of resources. This means that the company should be able to increase its revenues significantly without a corresponding increase in operational costs.

There are several types of scalable revenue models:

Subscription-Based Models: Subscription models, like those used by Netflix and Spotify, allow companies to generate recurring revenue from a large customer base. As more users subscribe to the service, the cost of delivering that service does not increase proportionally, making the business highly scalable.

Platform-Based Models: Platforms like Amazon and eBay connect buyers and sellers, creating a marketplace where the platform owner earns revenue through transaction fees or commissions. These platforms scale easily as more users join, without significantly increasing costs.

Freemium Models: Companies like LinkedIn and Dropbox use freemium models, offering basic services for free while charging for premium features. This allows for rapid customer acquisition at minimal cost, with the potential to monetize a percentage of users over time.

The revenue model chosen must align with the company's overall strategy and support long-term growth.

c. Operational Efficiency

Scalability requires operational efficiency. As a company grows, it must optimize its internal processes to handle increased demand without bottlenecks or inefficiencies. This means that the business must invest in systems and infrastructure that can scale along with the company.

To achieve operational efficiency, businesses should:

Automate Routine Processes: Automation reduces manual intervention in routine tasks like invoicing, customer support, and inventory management. For instance, cloud-based software like Salesforce or SAP helps companies manage customer relationships, track sales, and optimize operations at scale.

Invest in Scalable Technology: Cloud computing, data analytics, and artificial intelligence (AI) are examples of technologies that support scalability. Cloud-based infrastructure allows companies to increase their computing capacity on-demand, while AI can optimize workflows and decision-making processes as the business grows.

Outsource Non-Core Activities: Outsourcing non-core activities such as logistics, IT support, or customer service to third-party providers can allow businesses to scale without overextending their internal resources.

d. Customer Acquisition and Retention

Customer acquisition is a critical component of scalability. However, acquiring new customers should not come at the cost of profitability. Scalable businesses focus on creating efficient customer acquisition strategies that minimize costs while maximizing reach.

Several strategies can help businesses scale their customer acquisition efforts:

Digital Marketing: Scalable businesses leverage digital marketing channels like social media, search engines, and email marketing to reach a wide audience at a relatively low cost. These channels allow for targeted marketing and personalized customer engagement, which increases the chances of conversion.

Referral Programs: Many scalable businesses use referral programs to encourage existing customers to bring in new customers. For example, Dropbox's referral program rewarded users with extra storage space for each successful referral, which helped the company grow exponentially.

Partnerships and Alliances: Forming strategic partnerships with other businesses can help scale customer acquisition by tapping into new markets or customer segments. Partnerships can also reduce the costs associated with entering new markets by leveraging the partner's existing infrastructure.

Customer retention is equally important for scalability. Businesses that retain customers through loyalty programs, excellent customer service, and personalized experiences can reduce churn and create a sustainable revenue stream.

e. Cost Structure and Profitability

A scalable business model must maintain a healthy balance between growth and profitability. While growth is essential, businesses must avoid overextending themselves and incurring unsustainable costs. The key is to develop a cost structure that supports scaling without compromising profitability.

Some strategies for achieving this include:

Economies of Scale: As a business grows, it should be able to reduce per-unit costs through economies of scale. This means that the cost of producing goods or delivering services decreases as the company increases its output.

Variable Costs vs. Fixed Costs: Scalable businesses often focus on minimizing fixed costs and relying more on variable costs. For example, companies that rely on cloud-based infrastructure incur costs based on usage, which allows them to scale operations without significant upfront investments.

Lean Operations: Lean business practices focus on reducing waste and improving efficiency. By eliminating unnecessary processes and optimizing resources, businesses can lower costs and improve scalability.

f. Adaptability and Flexibility

The ability to adapt to changing market conditions is a hallmark of scalable businesses. Companies that are rigid in their approach often struggle to scale because they cannot respond to new opportunities or challenges. Scalable businesses are flexible in their operations, allowing them to pivot when necessary, explore new markets, or adjust their strategies based on customer feedback or industry trends.

Being adaptable means having a business model that can evolve over time. Companies like Amazon started as online booksellers but adapted their model to become one of the world's largest e-commerce platforms by identifying new opportunities and expanding their offerings.

Case Studies of Scalable Business Models

To better understand how these principles apply in the real world, let's examine a few case studies of companies that have successfully built scalable business models.

Uber

Uber's business model is an excellent example of scalability. The company operates a platform that connects drivers with passengers, but it does not own any vehicles. This allows Uber to scale rapidly without the capital investment required to own and maintain a fleet of cars. As Uber expanded globally, it leveraged local regulations and market dynamics to adapt its model to different regions, further enhancing its scalability.

Airbnb

Airbnb similarly operates a platform-based business model that connects property owners with travelers. Like Uber, Airbnb does not own any properties, which allows it to scale quickly without the overhead costs of managing physical assets. The company also uses data analytics to optimize its platform, providing personalized recommendations to users and improving the overall customer experience.

Building a scalable business model is crucial for long-term success in today's competitive environment. By focusing on creating a strong value proposition, optimizing revenue models, ensuring operational efficiency, and maintaining flexibility, businesses can position themselves for sustained growth. Scalability is not just about expanding rapidly; it is about growing efficiently and sustainably while maximizing profitability. Companies that build with scalability in mind will be better equipped to seize opportunities, overcome challenges, and achieve long-term success.

CHAPTER TWO

LEAN STRATEGIES FOR SUSTAINABLE BUSINESS GROWTH

Introduction to Lean Principles in Business Growth

Lean strategies, initially developed in manufacturing by Toyota, have expanded into numerous industries as a framework for achieving sustainable business growth. The core principles of lean thinking revolve around maximizing customer value while minimizing waste. By focusing on delivering value more efficiently, businesses can grow sustainably without unnecessary costs or resource use, leading to more profitability and adaptability in dynamic markets.

Lean approaches are designed to streamline operations, eliminate non-value-adding activities, and ensure continuous improvement. These principles are vital for businesses seeking sustainable growth because they focus on long-term efficiencies rather than short-term gains. By using lean methods, businesses not only increase their operational efficiency but also create a more adaptable and resilient organization, capable of responding to market shifts and scaling effectively.

Eliminating Waste to Optimize Resources

One of the foundational elements of lean strategy is eliminating waste, known as "Muda" in lean terminology. Waste can take various forms, such as unnecessary production, excessive inventory, delays, or inefficient processes. Lean strategies focus on identifying and removing these inefficiencies to free up resources and improve productivity.

Types of Waste in Business Operations

　　i.　**Overproduction:** Producing more than is needed or before it is needed.

　　ii.　**Waiting:** Time wasted when resources are not being fully utilized.

　　iii.　**Transport**: Unnecessary movement of products or information.

　　iv.　**Overprocessing**: Performing more work or using more materials than necessary.

　　v.　**Inventory**: Excess products or materials not being processed.

vi. **Defects:** Effort involved in inspecting and fixing errors or poor-quality goods.

To implement lean effectively, companies use tools like Value Stream Mapping and 5S (Sort, Set in Order, Shine, Standardize, Sustain) to create a clear picture of how value flows through the organization and identify areas for improvement. Streamlining processes and cutting down on waste can improve efficiency, speed up production cycles, and reduce costs, leading to more sustainable growth.

Building a Customer-Centric Approach

At the heart of lean strategies is the idea of creating value for the customer. A lean business constantly strives to understand and meet customer needs without over-delivering or under-delivering. Lean companies focus on what customers truly value and work to eliminate any processes or activities that do not directly contribute to customer satisfaction.

Creating Customer-Centric Products and Services

Businesses must continually engage with their customers to gain insights into what they value most. Lean product development emphasizes starting with the most basic version of a product that fulfills customer needs, known as the Minimum Viable Product (MVP). By releasing this MVP, companies can gather real-time feedback from customers, making improvements and adjustments based on actual usage rather than assumptions. This customer-first approach minimizes waste in product development and ensures that the company's efforts are aligned with market demand.

Lean Product Development for Sustainable Growth

By using lean principles in product development, companies can innovate faster and more efficiently. Reducing the time and resources spent on features or products that don't provide value allows companies to focus on initiatives that support growth and profitability. Companies can scale more effectively by ensuring that their products and services are directly aligned with what the market wants.

Continuous Improvement through Kaizen

Lean strategies emphasize Kaizen, which means "continuous improvement." This principle encourages small, incremental changes that accumulate over time to create significant improvements. Rather than relying on large, disruptive changes, lean organizations foster a culture where every employee is empowered to contribute ideas for improving processes, reducing waste, and enhancing customer value.

Implementing Continuous Feedback Loops

In a lean organization, feedback loops are essential for sustaining continuous improvement. Companies gather insights from customers, employees, and processes, making adjustments as needed. By regularly evaluating performance and making small improvements, lean organizations can remain agile and competitive in the market.

Kaizen involves everyone in the organization, from leadership to frontline workers, in the pursuit of operational excellence. This democratic approach to problem-solving ensures that innovation and efficiency are ongoing processes rather than occasional events. Lean companies that adopt Kaizen as a core value see improvements in both employee morale and operational efficiency, leading to long-term sustainable growth.

Lean Leadership and Organizational Culture

Leadership plays a critical role in the successful implementation of lean strategies. Lean leadership is not about controlling every aspect of the business but about fostering an environment where continuous improvement is part of the organizational culture. Leaders in a lean organization set the vision, remove barriers to improvement, and empower employees to take ownership of their roles in the growth process.

Fostering a Lean Mindset

To create a lean culture, leadership must model the behaviors they want to see in the organization. This means prioritizing customer value, seeking efficiency, and always looking for ways to eliminate waste. A lean mindset also encourages a focus on long-term goals over short-term gains, which is crucial for sustainable growth.

Leadership's Role in Sustainable Lean Practices

Leaders must also be champions of lean tools and methods. They need to ensure that their teams are properly trained in lean practices and that they have the resources necessary to make improvements. By fostering a culture of continuous improvement, leaders help ensure that the business remains agile and capable of scaling efficiently as it grows.

Lean Supply Chain Management

Supply chain management is a critical area where lean strategies can drive growth. In a traditional supply chain, excess inventory, long lead times, and inefficient processes can tie up resources and limit scalability. A lean supply chain focuses on delivering products just in time, reducing waste, and optimizing the flow of goods and services.

Just-in-Time Delivery and Procurement

The Just-in-Time (JIT) system, a key component of lean supply chain management, involves producing and delivering products only as they are needed. This reduces the need for excessive inventory and helps companies respond more quickly to changes in demand.

Lean Financial Management for Sustainable Growth

Applying lean principles to financial management can also drive sustainable growth. Lean finance involves identifying and eliminating financial waste, ensuring that capital is allocated to the most impactful activities, and improving the efficiency of financial processes.

Managing Cash Flow through Lean Principles

Lean companies focus on maintaining strong cash flow by minimizing unnecessary expenses, optimizing working capital, and reducing financial waste. By keeping financial operations lean, companies can reinvest in growth and ensure long-term sustainability.

Lean Marketing and Customer Acquisition

Marketing can be a costly function, but lean strategies allow businesses to acquire customers more efficiently and cost-effectively. Lean marketing focuses on data-driven decisions, low-cost, high-impact strategies, and building customer loyalty through targeted engagement.

Low-Cost, High-Impact Marketing Strategies

Lean marketing emphasizes tactics like growth hacking, which uses creativity, analytical thinking, and social metrics to gain exposure and acquire customers quickly. These strategies often rely on digital platforms, making them more scalable and cost-effective than traditional marketing approaches.

Lean Innovation and Product Development

Innovation is at the heart of lean strategies. By focusing on rapid prototyping and testing, lean companies can bring products to market faster and with less risk. The use of Minimal Viable Products (MVP) allows companies to iterate quickly based on customer feedback, avoiding the waste of developing features or products that customers don't need or want.

Scaling Lean Strategies for Long-Term Success

As businesses grow, scaling lean strategies becomes essential. Maintaining lean efficiency while expanding operations requires a careful balance of automation, delegation, and process refinement. Case studies of companies that have successfully scaled using lean principles, like Toyota and Amazon, demonstrate that a commitment to lean thinking can drive sustained success in larger organizations.

Lean Strategies for a Sustainable Future

Lean strategies offer a roadmap for businesses looking to achieve sustainable growth by eliminating waste, improving efficiency, and staying focused on delivering customer value. By integrating lean principles into every aspect of the business, from leadership and culture to supply chain management and innovation, companies can build a foundation for long-term success. The lean approach is not just a set of tools but a mindset that ensures the business remains agile, responsive, and scalable in an ever-changing market.

Benefits of Lean Approaches for Growth

Lean approaches offer numerous benefits for business growth, providing companies with a framework for achieving sustainable, efficient, and profitable expansion. Below are some of the key advantages:

a. Operational Efficiency

Lean approaches focus on eliminating waste and optimizing processes, which leads to greater efficiency in operations. By identifying and removing activities that do not add value, businesses can streamline their workflows, reduce production times, and increase output without requiring additional resources. This allows companies to operate more efficiently, even as they grow, without compromising quality.

b. Cost Reduction

One of the core principles of lean thinking is reducing waste in all forms, including overproduction, excess inventory, and unnecessary labor. By cutting out these inefficiencies, businesses can significantly reduce operational costs. Lean approaches help companies focus resources on areas that contribute directly to customer value, leading to cost savings that can be reinvested into growth initiatives.

c. Faster Time-to-Market

Lean strategies emphasize rapid iteration, particularly through the development of Minimal Viable Products (MVPs) and continuous feedback loops. By focusing on delivering value quickly and iterating based on customer input, businesses can bring products and services to market faster. This agility gives companies a competitive edge, allowing them to capitalize on opportunities and adapt to changes in demand or market conditions.

d. Improved Product Quality

Lean approaches encourage a focus on continuous improvement, or Kaizen, where every process is constantly evaluated for potential enhancements. This philosophy not only improves operational efficiency but also ensures that product quality is continuously refined. Regular feedback from customers, coupled with iterative product development, helps companies better align their offerings with customer needs, resulting in higher satisfaction and fewer defects.

e. Enhanced Customer Satisfaction

By concentrating on creating value for the customer and eliminating non-value-adding activities, lean approaches help businesses develop products and services that better meet customer expectations. Lean's emphasis on understanding customer needs and quickly responding to feedback ensures that companies remain customer-focused, leading to improved satisfaction and loyalty.

Eliminating Waste to Optimize Resources

In the context of lean strategies, the concept of eliminating waste, also known as "Muda" in Japanese lean terminology, is a critical element in optimizing resources and driving sustainable growth. Waste refers to any activity or process that does not add value to the customer or the business, and eliminating it allows companies to focus their resources on activities that contribute directly to creating value. By reducing waste, businesses can improve efficiency, reduce costs, and enhance overall productivity.

There are seven types of waste commonly identified in lean methodology, each of which presents an opportunity for resource optimization:

a. Overproduction

Overproduction occurs when more products or services are created than what is needed or produced before they are required by the customer. This type of waste often leads to excess inventory, higher storage costs, and the risk of obsolescence. It ties up valuable resources in unnecessary production, which could otherwise be used more effectively.

How to Eliminate Overproduction:

i. Use demand forecasting to match production levels with actual customer needs.

ii. Implement Just-in-Time (JIT) production systems, which ensure that products are only made when they are needed.

iii. Focus on creating flexible production processes that can respond quickly to changes in demand.

b. Waiting

Waiting waste happens when workers, machinery, or materials are idle due to delays in the process. This can occur because of bottlenecks, inefficient scheduling, or unbalanced workloads, resulting in wasted time and productivity.

How to Eliminate Waiting:

i. Use better scheduling and resource management tools to ensure smoother transitions between tasks.

ii. Apply lean principles like load balancing to distribute work evenly across teams and machinery.

iii. Implement process automation and real-time monitoring to reduce downtime.

c. Transport

Transportation waste refers to the unnecessary movement of materials or products from one place to another within a facility or supply chain. Each instance of transportation adds time and cost but does not add value to the product.

How to Eliminate Transportation Waste:

i. Reorganize the layout of workspaces to minimize the distance products or materials need to travel.

ii. Use lean tools like Value Stream Mapping (VSM) to identify and reduce unnecessary movement in production or delivery processes.

iii. Work with suppliers to optimize logistics and ensure materials arrive when and where they are needed.

d. Overprocessing

Overprocessing occurs when more work is done on a product than is required to meet customer needs. This could involve using higher-quality materials than necessary, over-engineering products, or adding unnecessary features. It leads to excessive use of time, labor, and resources without providing additional value to the customer.

How to Eliminate Overprocessing:

i. Standardize processes to focus on customer requirements and avoid unnecessary steps or excessive quality control.

ii. Use lean product design principles to simplify products and focus only on essential features that provide value.

iii. Streamline approval processes and reduce redundant quality checks that do not contribute to customer satisfaction.

e. Inventory

Excess inventory is a form of waste because it ties up capital in materials that are not yet needed for production or delivery. This waste leads to additional storage costs and the risk of damage, spoilage, or obsolescence. Holding too much inventory also means that businesses are slow to respond to changes in customer demand.

How to Eliminate Inventory Waste:

i. Implement Just-in-Time (JIT) inventory systems to reduce stock levels and ensure that materials are available only when needed.

ii. Use inventory management tools and real-time tracking to optimize stock levels based on demand forecasting.

iii. Improve supplier relationships to ensure reliable and timely deliveries, reducing the need to hold excess inventory.

f. Motion

i. Motion waste refers to unnecessary movement of people, such as employees walking back and forth to retrieve tools, parts, or information. Excessive motion increases the time needed to complete tasks and can lead to employee fatigue and safety risks.

How to Eliminate Motion Waste:

i. Design workstations and production lines with ergonomics in mind, ensuring that tools and materials are easily accessible.

ii. Organize and standardize workflows to minimize unnecessary movements.

iii. Implement lean workplace organization techniques like 5S (Sort, Set in Order, Shine, Standardize, Sustain) to create more efficient work environments.

g. Defects

Defects represent the most obvious form of waste, as they lead to rework, repairs, or scrapping of products that fail to meet quality standards. Defective products not only waste materials but also consume additional labor, time, and resources in fixing or replacing them. Poor quality can also damage customer satisfaction and brand reputation.

How to Eliminate Defects:

i. Implement quality control measures at every stage of the process, ensuring that issues are identified and resolved early.

ii. Use root cause analysis tools like 5 Whys or Fishbone Diagrams to understand and eliminate the underlying causes of defects.

iii. Foster a culture of continuous improvement, where employees are encouraged to identify and fix quality issues as they arise.

Tools for Eliminating Waste in Business Operations

To effectively identify and eliminate waste, companies can use various lean tools, such as:

i. Value Stream Mapping (VSM): This tool helps businesses visualize the entire production or service delivery process, from start to finish, identifying any steps that do not add value.

ii. 5S System: A workplace organization method that helps improve efficiency by organizing tools, materials, and equipment to reduce waste in motion, waiting, and transport.

iii. Kaizen: A continuous improvement philosophy that empowers employees to suggest and implement small, incremental changes that reduce waste and improve processes over time.

iv. Kanban: A visual scheduling system that helps optimize the flow of work by ensuring that only necessary tasks are completed at any given time, reducing overproduction and waiting waste.

The Benefits of Eliminating Waste

Eliminating waste through lean strategies allows businesses to optimize their resources, leading to increased efficiency, cost savings, and improved profitability. By focusing on value-added activities, companies can enhance productivity, reduce operational costs, and become more agile and responsive to customer needs. This optimization ultimately contributes to sustainable growth, enabling businesses to scale effectively while maintaining high levels of quality and customer satisfaction.

Building a Customer-Centric Approach

In today's highly competitive and dynamic business environment, a customer-centric approach is no longer just a buzzword, but a vital strategy that ensures long-term success. It focuses on placing the customer at the heart of every business decision and action, resulting in enhanced customer satisfaction, loyalty, and ultimately, profitability. This approach requires an organizational shift from simply selling products or services to creating meaningful experiences that meet customers' evolving needs and preferences. In this extensive guide, we will delve into the key principles, benefits, and steps involved in building a customer-centric approach.

1. Understanding Customer-Centricity

A customer-centric approach involves deeply understanding customers, anticipating their needs, and delivering products and services that offer real value. Unlike product-centric models, which focus solely on the product or service, customer-centric organizations prioritize building strong relationships by delivering personalized experiences at every touchpoint.

This strategy requires aligning every department, from sales to marketing to customer support, toward the goal of satisfying the customer. It is driven by a company-wide culture that prioritizes customer insights, feedback, and engagement.

2. Key Principles of a Customer-Centric Approach

To effectively build a customer-centric model, there are several key principles that organizations should adopt:

i. Deep Customer Understanding

Customer-centric businesses invest heavily in understanding their customers' pain points, preferences, and behaviors. This can be achieved through methods such as customer interviews, surveys, and social listening. Customer data analytics also play a crucial role in identifying trends and anticipating future needs.

ii. Personalization

Modern consumers expect personalized experiences, whether in product recommendations, marketing messages, or customer service interactions. Companies that leverage customer data and insights to offer tailored solutions are more likely to stand out and build loyalty.

iii. Consistency Across Channels

In a multi-channel world, customers interact with brands across different touchpoints – in stores, online, via mobile apps, and on social media. A customer-centric approach ensures that each interaction provides a seamless and consistent experience, regardless of the channel. Omnichannel strategies are essential in delivering a unified brand experience.

iv. Proactive Problem-Solving

Customer-centric businesses anticipate potential problems and provide solutions before customers even recognize them. This proactive approach not only resolves issues swiftly but also demonstrates that the company genuinely cares about the customer's experience.

v. Feedback Integration

Constantly seeking and integrating customer feedback into product development and service improvement is a core tenet of customer-centricity. Businesses must treat feedback as a valuable asset and act on it promptly.

3. The Benefits of Adopting a Customer-Centric Approach

Transitioning to a customer-centric model comes with significant benefits for both businesses and their customers. Some of the notable advantages include:

i. Increased Customer Loyalty

By putting customers first and consistently exceeding their expectations, businesses can foster loyalty, turning one-time buyers into repeat customers. Loyal customers not only contribute to regular revenue streams but also become brand advocates, bringing in new customers through word-of-mouth.

ii. Higher Customer Lifetime Value (CLTV)

Customer-centric organizations increase the lifetime value of their customers by focusing on retention and long-term relationships. When customers feel valued and their needs are continuously met, they are more likely to return, make additional purchases, and stay loyal for longer periods.

iii. Improved Customer Satisfaction

Happy customers are more likely to share positive experiences and refer others to the business. By prioritizing customer satisfaction, companies can create positive brand associations and differentiate themselves from competitors.

iv. Competitive Advantage

In a crowded marketplace, businesses that excel in delivering exceptional customer experiences stand out. Customer-centric companies are more agile, adaptive, and responsive to changing customer needs, giving them a significant edge over competitors that fail to prioritize their customers.

v. Sustainable Growth

A customer-centric model drives sustainable business growth by fostering loyalty, attracting new customers, and enhancing brand reputation. With long-term customer relationships, businesses can weather market fluctuations and thrive in the long run.

4. Steps to Building a Customer-Centric Approach

To successfully implement a customer-centric approach, businesses need to follow these key steps:

i. Develop a Customer-Centric Culture

Creating a customer-first culture is the foundation of any successful customer-centric strategy. This involves ensuring that every employee, from leadership to frontline staff, is aligned with the goal of delivering exceptional customer experiences. It's essential for leaders to lead by example, instilling the importance of customer satisfaction throughout the organization.

Regular training sessions, workshops, and recognition programs can reinforce the customer-centric mindset. Employees who understand the value of customer satisfaction are more motivated to deliver quality service.

ii. Leverage Customer Data

To make informed decisions and provide personalized experiences, businesses must leverage data analytics to understand customer behavior, preferences, and needs. Data-driven insights can guide product development, marketing strategies, and customer service efforts.

Implementing tools like Customer Relationship Management (CRM) systems enables businesses to track customer interactions, identify trends, and personalize communication.

iii. Empower Employees to Make Decisions

Frontline employees, such as customer service representatives, should be empowered to resolve issues and make decisions without needing constant managerial approval. This empowerment fosters quicker problem resolution and demonstrates to customers that the company values their time and experience.

iv. Measure Customer Experience Metrics

Implementing metrics to assess customer experience is critical in ensuring that the customer-centric approach is working effectively. Metrics such as Net Promoter Score (NPS), Customer Satisfaction (CSAT), and Customer Effort Score (CES) can provide valuable insights into customer satisfaction levels and areas for improvement.

Regularly analyzing these metrics can help businesses refine their strategies, address weak points, and continuously enhance customer experiences.

v. Personalize Customer Interactions

Personalization is at the heart of customer-centricity. Whether it's through marketing emails, product recommendations, or customer service interactions, businesses should use customer data to tailor every interaction. Customers appreciate when businesses understand their unique preferences and cater to them individually.

vi. Create a Seamless Omnichannel Experience

Customers interact with brands through various channels, and they expect consistency across all of them. Whether a customer is browsing the website, using a mobile app, or speaking with customer support, their experience should be seamless.

An omnichannel strategy ensures that customers receive the same level of service and satisfaction, regardless of the platform they use. For instance, if a customer starts a conversation on social media, they should be able to continue it via email or phone without needing to repeat themselves.

5. Challenges in Adopting a Customer-Centric Approach

While the benefits of a customer-centric strategy are clear, businesses may face several challenges in implementing it. These include:

i. Cultural Resistance

Shifting to a customer-centric approach often requires a change in organizational culture, which can be met with resistance. Employees may be accustomed to product-focused or sales-driven models and might struggle to adopt a new mindset that prioritizes customer needs.

ii. Data Management

Effectively leveraging customer data is essential for personalization and insight-driven decision-making, but managing large volumes of data can be challenging. Businesses must ensure they have the right tools and systems in place to collect, analyze, and act on customer data.

iii. Cross-Departmental Alignment

A customer-centric approach requires collaboration across all departments, including marketing, sales, product development, and customer service. However, siloed departments can hinder the flow of customer information, making it difficult to deliver a unified experience.

Building a customer-centric approach is a transformative strategy that can drive long-term success in a competitive market. By focusing on deep customer understanding, personalization, and consistent experiences across all touchpoints, businesses can cultivate loyalty, enhance customer satisfaction, and differentiate themselves from competitors. While challenges may arise, the benefits far outweigh the difficulties, making customer-centricity a crucial investment for any organization looking to thrive in the modern business landscape.

Understanding Customer Needs and Value

Understanding customer needs and value is a cornerstone of any successful business strategy. It enables companies to develop products and services that truly resonate with their target audience, while also fostering long-term relationships built on trust and satisfaction. In this in-depth exploration, we will cover the importance of understanding customer needs, how businesses can identify and meet these needs, and the role that customer value plays in driving success.

The Importance of Understanding Customer Needs

At the heart of every business are the customers it serves. Customers come with their own unique preferences, problems, and expectations, and businesses must understand these needs to deliver relevant solutions. A deep understanding of customer needs ensures that businesses:

i. Develop Relevant Products and Services: By identifying customer needs, businesses can create offerings that solve real problems and enhance the customer's life. This reduces the risk of misalignment between what the company offers and what the market actually demands.

ii. Improve Customer Satisfaction: Meeting customer needs effectively results in higher satisfaction levels, which leads to customer loyalty, positive word-of-mouth referrals, and repeat business.

iii. Increase Competitive Advantage: In a crowded market, businesses that best understand their customers' needs have a competitive edge. They are able to innovate in ways that competitors might not, staying ahead by offering unique solutions.

iv. Optimize Marketing and Sales Efforts: When a business understands the core motivations of its target audience, it can tailor its marketing messages and sales pitches to better connect with customers and guide them through the purchase journey.

Types of Customer Needs

Understanding customer needs goes beyond the surface level. Customers often have a range of needs that can be categorized in different ways:

a. Basic Needs

Basic needs refer to the essential requirements that customers expect from a product or service. These needs must be fulfilled for a customer to consider a purchase. For example, in a smartphone, basic needs would include reliable connectivity, a user-friendly interface, and adequate storage space.

b. Performance Needs

These needs are tied to the performance or functionality of the product or service. Customers assess the value based on how well the product meets their expectations for performance. For instance, how fast the phone processes tasks or how clear the camera quality is.

c. Unstated Needs

Sometimes, customers have needs that they do not explicitly voice, but they expect businesses to understand and address. A customer might not ask for an intuitive user experience but still expects the product to be easy to use without hassle.

d. Delight Needs

These are additional features or services that exceed customer expectations and enhance the overall experience. These needs go beyond what is expected and offer a "wow" factor, such as exceptional customer service, a personalized experience, or additional features that make the product stand out.

e. Latent Needs

Latent needs are those that customers may not be aware of themselves, but once the need is fulfilled, they recognize its value. Innovative companies often uncover latent needs through research and development, offering breakthrough solutions that revolutionize the customer experience.

How to Identify Customer Needs

Successfully identifying customer needs requires a combination of qualitative and quantitative research methods. Businesses must gather direct insights from customers and also analyze market data to draw conclusions. Some effective ways to identify customer needs include:

a. Customer Interviews and Surveys

Directly asking customers about their experiences, pain points, and preferences is a highly effective way to understand their needs. Surveys can capture both qualitative and quantitative data, while interviews allow for in-depth exploration of individual customer experiences.

b. Social Listening

Monitoring conversations on social media platforms, forums, and review sites gives businesses a real-time pulse on what customers are saying about their products and services, as well as competitors'. Social listening tools can help companies track sentiment, identify recurring themes, and uncover new areas of opportunity.

c. Customer Feedback and Support Data

Customer service interactions, feedback forms, and support requests provide invaluable information about recurring problems or areas where customers feel underserved. Analyzing customer feedback allows companies to spot patterns and areas for improvement.

d. Behavioral Data Analysis

By examining customer behavior on websites, apps, and in-store, businesses can identify unmet needs. For example, if customers frequently abandon their shopping carts at a certain step, it could indicate friction in the checkout process. Behavioral data analysis helps businesses optimize user experience and address potential roadblocks.

e. Competitive Analysis

Studying competitors' offerings and understanding how they address customer needs can reveal gaps in the market. A competitor might offer a feature or benefit that resonates well with customers, indicating an opportunity to innovate or improve.

Meeting Customer Needs

Once customer needs are identified, the next step is to meet them effectively. Here are key strategies businesses can adopt to fulfill customer needs and add value:

a. Product and Service Customization

Personalization is a powerful way to meet customer needs. Businesses can use customer data to create tailored offerings that suit individual preferences. For example, in the e-commerce space, companies use algorithms to recommend products based on past purchases and browsing history.

b. Improving User Experience

User experience (UX) plays a critical role in customer satisfaction. Whether it's a digital interface, a physical product, or a service interaction, businesses should ensure that the experience is intuitive, seamless, and enjoyable. Continuous improvements based on customer feedback and testing can help refine the experience.

c. Customer-Centric Innovation

Businesses that consistently innovate with the customer in mind can stay ahead of competitors. Customer-centric innovation involves developing new products, services, or features that directly address unmet or latent needs, often resulting in breakthrough solutions that delight customers.

d. Exceptional Customer Service

Meeting customer needs extends beyond the product or service itself. Offering exceptional customer support through multiple channels, quick response times, and problem resolution are vital elements of a customer-centric approach. Customers appreciate when businesses are proactive and responsive to their concerns.

e. Value-Based Pricing

Customers often assess the value of a product based on its price. Pricing strategies should reflect the perceived value the customer derives from the product or service. Offering tiered pricing, bundles, or value-added services can meet different customer segments' needs while enhancing their overall satisfaction.

Understanding Customer Value

Customer value is the perception of the worth or benefit a customer receives from a product or service relative to its cost. It's not just about the price but also the overall experience, quality, and emotional satisfaction a customer gains. Businesses that maximize customer value often experience higher retention rates, stronger brand loyalty, and increased profitability.

a. Functional Value

This refers to the utility or performance the product or service offers. For example, a vacuum cleaner's functional value might be measured by its suction power and ability to clean various surfaces.

b. Emotional Value

Emotional value comes from the positive feelings a customer associates with a product or brand. This could be driven by the brand's reputation, customer service, or even the pride or joy a customer feels when using the product.

c. Social Value

Social value arises when a product helps customers enhance their social standing or fit into a desired social group. For instance, certain brands of luxury goods or technology products may be perceived as status symbols.

d. Economic Value

Economic value reflects the financial benefit a customer derives from a product or service, such as cost savings, discounts, or long-term durability that reduces the need for frequent replacements.

Delivering and Enhancing Customer Value

To deliver customer value effectively, businesses should focus on several key areas:

a. Understanding the Customer's Perspective

What one customer values may differ from what another values. It's essential for businesses to segment their audience and understand what drives value for each segment. A tech-savvy customer may value advanced features, while another may prioritize ease of use.

b. Communicating Value

A product's value must be clearly communicated to customers. Businesses should focus on highlighting the benefits and outcomes that customers will experience rather than just the features of the product. Effective marketing and sales messages should resonate with the target audience's needs and desires.

c. Consistent Value Delivery

Consistency is critical in delivering customer value. Whether it's the quality of the product, the level of service, or the overall experience, customers expect businesses to deliver on their promises time and time again. Failure to meet these expectations can lead to dissatisfaction and churn.

d. Continuous Improvement

Customer value is not static. Businesses must continually seek ways to enhance the value they offer through innovation, improvements in product quality, better customer support, or additional services. Customer feedback and market trends should guide these improvements.

Understanding customer needs and delivering value is the foundation of building a successful and sustainable business. By deeply understanding what drives customer behavior, addressing unmet needs, and consistently delivering value, businesses can build strong, lasting relationships with their customers. In turn, customers will reward these efforts with loyalty, positive reviews, and continued patronage, creating a cycle of growth and success.

Lean Leadership and Organizational Culture

Lean leadership and organizational culture are two pivotal aspects of business management that have a profound influence on a company's overall performance, efficiency, and ability to innovate. Lean leadership, rooted in the principles of lean manufacturing and continuous improvement, emphasizes eliminating waste, improving processes, and maximizing value for customers. Meanwhile, organizational culture refers to the shared values, beliefs, and norms that shape how people within an organization behave and interact.

When lean leadership is aligned with a supportive organizational culture, it can drive remarkable operational improvements, employee engagement, and long-term success. In this comprehensive book, we will explore the principles of lean leadership, the role of organizational culture, and how the two work together to create high-performing organizations.

Principles of Lean Leadership

Lean leadership is based on the principles of lean manufacturing, first popularized by Toyota's production system. It focuses on fostering a culture of continuous improvement (often referred to as "Kaizen"), empowering employees, and driving efficiency by eliminating waste (referred to as "muda" in lean terms). The key principles of lean leadership include:

a. Respect for People

Lean leadership begins with respect for employees at all levels of the organization. Leaders must create an environment where employees feel valued, trusted, and empowered to make decisions. This principle encourages collaboration, open communication, and a shared commitment to achieving business goals.

b. Focus on Continuous Improvement

A core element of lean leadership is the relentless pursuit of improvement. Leaders encourage their teams to constantly identify inefficiencies and opportunities for optimization. This can involve improving processes, reducing waste, enhancing quality, or innovating new ways to deliver value to customers.

c. Elimination of Waste

One of the primary goals of lean leadership is to reduce or eliminate waste in all its forms. Waste in lean terms refers to anything that does not add value to the customer. This includes unnecessary steps in processes, excess inventory, overproduction, and underutilization of talent. Lean leaders guide their teams in streamlining operations to focus on value-adding activities.

d. Empowering Employees

Lean leadership shifts the decision-making power closer to where the work is done. Employees who are directly involved in processes often have the best insights into where improvements can be made. By empowering employees to take ownership of their work and make decisions, lean leaders cultivate a sense of responsibility and innovation across the organization.

e. Value Stream Focus

Lean leadership emphasizes understanding and optimizing the entire value stream—the sequence of activities involved in delivering a product or service to the customer. Leaders focus on ensuring that each step in the value stream adds value and supports the overall mission of delivering high-quality products or services efficiently.

f. Leader as a Teacher and Coach

In lean organizations, leaders take on the role of coaches and teachers, guiding their teams toward self-improvement. Rather than simply dictating tasks, lean leaders mentor employees, helping them develop problem-solving skills and take ownership of continuous improvement initiatives. This approach fosters a learning culture within the organization.

The Role of Organizational Culture

Organizational culture refers to the shared values, behaviors, and practices that shape how employees interact with each other and how they approach their work. It can be seen as the "personality" of the organization and plays a crucial role in determining how well lean principles can be implemented and sustained. A culture that supports lean leadership is essential for the long-term success of lean initiatives.

a. Values and Beliefs

The underlying values and beliefs of an organization form the foundation of its culture. In a lean organization, these values are likely to include a commitment to quality, customer focus, respect for people, and continuous improvement. Employees in a lean culture believe that their work matters and that they have the ability to influence positive change.

b. Collaboration and Teamwork

Lean organizations foster a collaborative culture where teamwork is valued. This is essential for identifying inefficiencies and driving improvements, as many process-related issues span multiple departments. In a lean culture, teams work together to solve problems, share knowledge, and support one another in achieving organizational goals.

c. Accountability and Ownership

In a lean culture, employees are encouraged to take ownership of their work and be accountable for their performance. This sense of accountability drives a culture of continuous improvement, as employees feel responsible for finding ways to enhance the efficiency and quality of their work.

d. Openness to Change

A lean organizational culture must be open to change. Lean leadership encourages employees to question the status quo, challenge outdated processes, and seek better ways of doing things. This requires a cultural shift away from rigid thinking and toward embracing innovation and adaptation.

e. Learning and Development

Continuous improvement requires a commitment to learning and development. In a lean culture, organizations invest in training employees to build their problem-solving and technical skills. A strong emphasis is placed on developing both individuals and teams to enhance their ability to identify and implement improvements.

f. Trust and Transparency

A lean organizational culture is built on trust and transparency. Leaders are open about challenges, goals, and expectations, and employees feel confident that their input is valued. Transparent communication between all levels of the organization creates a supportive environment where employees are willing to share ideas and collaborate on solutions.

How Lean Leadership and Organizational Culture Work Together

Lean leadership and organizational culture are interdependent. A supportive organizational culture is essential for lean leadership to thrive, and lean leadership, in turn, reinforces the positive aspects of organizational culture. Together, they create a framework that drives continuous improvement, innovation, and operational excellence. Below are key ways in which lean leadership and organizational culture intersect:

a. Fostering Employee Engagement

Lean leadership places a high value on employee involvement, which is reinforced by an organizational culture that promotes respect, trust, and empowerment. When employees feel engaged and empowered, they are more likely to contribute ideas for improvement and take ownership of their roles. This mutual reinforcement drives high levels of engagement and performance.

b. Creating a Problem-Solving Culture

In lean organizations, leaders encourage employees to identify and solve problems. This requires a culture where employees are not only comfortable voicing concerns but are also equipped with the skills to address them. A culture that promotes continuous learning, innovation, and open communication is crucial for building a problem-solving mindset.

c. Building Long-Term Sustainability

For lean initiatives to be sustainable, the organizational culture must support continuous improvement over the long term. A lean culture values incremental progress and fosters a mindset of "learning by doing." Lean leaders play a pivotal role in embedding this mindset across the organization, ensuring that improvements are sustained and that the organization remains adaptable to change.

d. Driving Innovation

Lean leadership encourages innovation through a focus on customer value, efficiency, and problem-solving. In an organization with a lean culture, employees are encouraged to experiment with new ideas, improve processes, and innovate in ways that add value. Leaders create an environment where calculated risks are rewarded and where experimentation is seen as part of the continuous improvement journey.

e. Improving Collaboration Across Functions

A lean organizational culture breaks down silos and encourages cross-functional collaboration. Lean leaders promote transparency and alignment across departments, ensuring that everyone is working toward the same goals. By creating a culture of shared responsibility and cooperation, lean leadership helps to streamline processes and improve overall efficiency.

f. Empowering Decision-Making at All Levels

One of the hallmarks of lean leadership is the delegation of decision-making to those closest to the work. This empowers employees to take action and make changes that will improve their work processes. In a culture that supports this kind of empowerment, employees feel trusted and are motivated to contribute their best efforts.

Challenges in Implementing Lean Leadership and Culture

While lean leadership and organizational culture can bring significant benefits, they are not without challenges. Implementing lean practices requires a cultural shift that may face resistance. Some common challenges include:

a. Resistance to Change

Cultural shifts can be met with resistance, particularly if employees are used to a more hierarchical or traditional leadership style. Lean leadership requires a more open and inclusive approach, which can be challenging for organizations with deeply entrenched power structures.

b. Short-Term Thinking

Lean leadership focuses on long-term, sustainable improvements, which may not always align with short-term business pressures. It requires patience and a willingness to invest in continuous improvement rather than seeking immediate results.

c. Maintaining Momentum

Sustaining a lean culture requires ongoing effort and leadership commitment. Without consistent support from leadership, the organization may revert to old habits and lose the gains achieved through lean initiatives.

d. Lack of Skills and Training

For lean leadership to succeed, employees need the right tools and training to participate in continuous improvement initiatives. Organizations that do not invest in developing their employees' problem-solving and analytical skills may struggle to fully implement lean principles.

Lean leadership and organizational culture are critical components in driving operational excellence, continuous improvement, and long-term success. By fostering a culture that promotes respect, collaboration, accountability, and innovation, organizations can create an environment where lean principles thrive. When lean leadership is aligned with a supportive organizational culture, the entire organization becomes more agile, efficient, and customer-focused, setting the stage for sustained growth and competitive advantage.

Effective lean leadership and the right cultural foundation empower employees at all levels to contribute to the organization's success, ensuring that improvements are not only implemented but also sustained over time.

CHAPTER THREE

DEVELOPING RESILIENT BUSSINESS MODELS IN UNCERTAIN MARKET

In the contemporary landscape, unpredictability has become a prevailing factor, with enterprises constantly encountering unforeseeable shifts in market conditions, consumer behavior, technological advancements, and global dynamics. Whether it be economic downturns, geopolitical unrest, natural calamities, or technological disruptions, organizations must be equipped to confront a diverse array of challenges that could jeopardize their operations. As volatility escalates, establishing resilient business models emerges as imperative for entities to withstand shocks, adapt to evolving circumstances, and seize emerging opportunities.

A resilient business model transcends mere survival; it positions a company to flourish in dynamic and often erratic environments. Such models enable organizations to promptly respond to disruptions, while cultivating long-term adaptability, flexibility, and robustness. By nurturing resilience, businesses can uphold competitiveness, foster continuous innovation, and effectively mitigate risks, all while sustaining profitability and relevance irrespective of market conditions. This exploration delves into the fundamental drivers behind the necessity for resilience, methodologies to cultivate it, and instances of companies that have adeptly navigated uncertain markets.

The Imperative for Resilient Business Models

The imperative for resilient business models has never been more conspicuous. Modern enterprises are operating within an increasingly intricate and unpredictable milieu. Conventional approaches that prioritize short-term efficiency or profitability at the expense of flexibility are proving insufficient in the face of rapidly shifting market dynamics. Below are some pivotal factors that underscore the exigency for resilient business models:

a. Globalization and Geopolitical Risks

As globalization has proliferated, markets have grown more intertwined, leaving businesses vulnerable to geopolitical risks and uncertainties. Political upheavals, trade disputes, or abrupt regulatory modifications in one region can swiftly generate global ramifications. For instance, a trade conflict between major economies can disrupt international supply chains, resulting in delays, cost escalations, or scarcities that impact businesses worldwide. To mitigate these risks, companies must exhibit agility, diversify their operations, and devise robust contingency plans.

b. Technological Disruption

The pace of technological evolution is accelerating, and enterprises that lag behind risk obsolescence. Disruptive technologies such as artificial intelligence (AI), automation, blockchain, and the Internet of Things (IoT) are reshaping entire industries. Companies that are excessively rigid or sluggish in adopting new technologies may find their business models becoming outmoded. A resilient business model must not only embrace innovation but also ensure swift adaptation to shifts catalyzed by technological advancements.

c. Economic Volatility

Economic instability, encompassing recessions, inflation, or currency fluctuations, engenders substantial uncertainty for businesses. Abrupt fluctuations in consumer demand, escalating operational expenses, or fluctuating interest rates can unsettle organizations overly reliant on stable economic conditions. Business resilience necessitates financial strategies that prioritize liquidity, diversify funding streams, and construct a buffer for navigating economic downturns, guaranteeing the organization's survival without resorting to detrimental measures that compromise its long-term viability.

d. Environmental and Climate Challenges

The mounting consciousness of environmental and climate-related risks is compelling businesses to reevaluate their models with a heightened emphasis on sustainability. Natural disasters like floods, hurricanes, and wildfires pose significant threats to supply chains, infrastructure, and operations. Moreover, stringent environmental regulations and the escalating demand for eco-friendly products are compelling companies to integrate sustainability into their strategies. Resilient businesses must not only address physical risks but also adapt to regulatory pressures and shifts in consumer behavior linked to environmental concerns.

In this context, developing a resilient business model is imperative for ensuring enduring success and stability in a world characterized by perpetual change.

Strategic Flexibility: Building Agility and Adaptability into Business Operations

Strategic flexibility is essential for companies aiming to not only survive but thrive in a rapidly evolving business environment. As markets experience volatility, organizations that prioritize agility and adaptability in their operations are better equipped to respond to unexpected changes and capitalize on emerging opportunities. Businesses must be able to pivot quickly in response to shifts in consumer preferences, technological disruptions, and supply chain challenges while maintaining operational efficiency.

Strategic flexibility encompasses the capacity of an organization to realign its objectives, resources, and processes in response to internal and external changes, all while preserving its overall vision and competitive edge. This concept involves creating an adaptable structure that fosters innovation and resilience. Below, we explore the core elements of strategic flexibility, its critical importance for modern businesses, and effective strategies to build agility and adaptability into operations.

Understanding Strategic Flexibility

Strategic flexibility is characterized by an organization's ability to respond effectively to changes in the business environment. It involves designing structures that anticipate change and integrate flexibility into the core operational processes. The goal is to create a system that can withstand shocks and seize new opportunities as they arise.

Key aspects of strategic flexibility include:

i. Dynamic decision-making processes that allow organizations to assess situations and make informed changes rapidly.

ii. Resource reallocation capabilities that enable the shifting of manpower, capital, and technology towards new priorities.

iii. Diversified business models that provide multiple pathways for growth and revenue, mitigating risks associated with dependency on a single line of business.

iv. Cultural adaptability where teams are encouraged to innovate and remain open to change, ensuring alignment with flexible goals.

The Importance of Agility and Adaptability in Operations

Agility and adaptability are crucial components of strategic flexibility, focusing on how quickly and easily a business can respond to market changes. Agile businesses are marked by swift decision-making, decentralized structures, and empowered teams that can execute changes without bureaucratic delays. Adaptability emphasizes the overall evolution of the business model, products, services, and processes in response to new challenges.

a. Agility in Decision-Making

Creating a structure that enables fast, informed decision-making is critical for building flexibility. Traditional hierarchies often slow down decision-making processes due to multiple levels of approval, which can hinder a company's ability to respond to rapidly changing conditions.

Companies that flatten their hierarchies and empower cross-functional teams can act more swiftly, maintaining a competitive edge. During market disruptions, businesses that rely on centralized decision-making may struggle to make timely adjustments, leading to missed opportunities or prolonged losses. In contrast, organizations that give managers and employees the authority to make real-time decisions, particularly at the operational level, can quickly pivot their strategies to mitigate risks.

b. Resource Allocation and Operational Shifts

Strategic flexibility requires efficient resource reallocation—whether in terms of financial, human, or technological resources. When a product line underperforms, flexible organizations can swiftly direct their resources towards more profitable areas or even pivot entirely to new product categories.

This process must occur smoothly to maintain business continuity. Companies can cultivate this capability by diversifying resource pools and ensuring that personnel are trained to handle different roles or adapt to various technologies. In the digital age, businesses must also develop the ability to adopt new tools and technologies quickly, enhancing operational efficiency.

c. Continuous Learning and Innovation

Fostering a culture of continuous learning and innovation is vital for maintaining flexibility. Organizations should encourage teams to seek improvements in processes, products, and services, giving employees the freedom to experiment and learn from failures.

This mindset ensures that companies remain open to new ideas and innovations that enhance adaptability.

Successful companies often invest in innovation labs or cross-functional teams focused on exploring new markets or technologies. These teams operate independently from the core business but provide critical insights and innovative solutions that can be integrated across the organization. When innovation is part of the corporate culture, employees become adept at handling change, driving agility across operations.

The Role of Technology in Building Agility

Technology is a pivotal factor in enhancing strategic flexibility. Digital transformation streamlines processes, improves communication, and enables quicker responses to market shifts. Several technological tools and systems support agility and adaptability in business operations.

a. Cloud Computing and Digital Infrastructure

Cloud computing has transformed business operations by offering scalable infrastructure that can adapt to market demands. This technology allows companies to deploy new services rapidly, access global markets, and respond to disruptions in real-time. The ability to scale operations—whether increasing capacity to meet demand spikes or scaling down to reduce costs—provides a significant advantage in uncertain markets.

b. Data Analytics for Informed Decision-Making

Advanced data analytics tools enable businesses to gather and analyze vast amounts of data to inform strategic decisions. By harnessing insights from customer behavior, market trends, and operational performance, organizations can identify opportunities for innovation and quickly adjust their strategies. This data-driven approach enhances agility by providing real-time insights that guide decision-making.

c. Collaboration Tools for Enhanced Communication

Effective communication is essential for maintaining agility within an organization. Collaboration tools and platforms facilitate seamless communication across teams, regardless of geographical locations. These tools enable real-time sharing of information and collaboration on projects, ensuring that teams can adapt quickly to changes and work together effectively.

Implementing Strategic Flexibility in Business Operations

To effectively implement strategic flexibility, organizations can adopt several best practices:

i. Cultivate a flexible organizational culture: Promote an environment where change is embraced, and employees are encouraged to think creatively and take calculated risks. This culture fosters innovation and prepares teams to adapt to new challenges.

ii. Invest in training and development: Provide continuous training opportunities for employees to enhance their skills and adapt to new technologies and processes. This investment ensures that the workforce is equipped to handle various roles and responsibilities.

iii. Establish cross-functional teams: Create teams composed of members from different departments to encourage diverse perspectives and collaboration. These teams can quickly address challenges and develop innovative solutions.

iv. Monitor market trends and consumer behavior: Stay informed about changes in the market landscape and consumer preferences. Regularly analyzing trends enables businesses to anticipate shifts and adapt proactively.

v. Foster partnerships and collaborations: Building strategic partnerships with other organizations can enhance flexibility by providing access to additional resources, expertise, and market insights.

Strategic flexibility is a vital component of a resilient business model, enabling organizations to navigate the complexities of uncertain markets. By prioritizing agility and adaptability, companies can respond to unexpected changes, innovate continuously, and ultimately thrive in an unpredictable environment. As the business landscape continues to evolve, fostering a culture of strategic flexibility will be essential for long-term success and competitiveness.

Managing Risks and Strengthening Financial Foundations

In an increasingly complex and uncertain business landscape, effective risk management and robust financial foundations are essential for organizations aiming to achieve sustainable growth and resilience. Companies face a myriad of risks, ranging from economic fluctuations and regulatory changes to technological disruptions and natural disasters. To navigate these challenges successfully, businesses must adopt comprehensive risk management strategies while simultaneously strengthening their financial stability.

This discussion explores the importance of managing risks and building strong financial foundations, key strategies for risk mitigation, and the role of financial resilience in supporting business longevity.

Understanding Risk Management

Risk management involves identifying, assessing, and prioritizing risks followed by the coordinated application of resources to minimize, monitor, and control the probability or impact of adverse events. Effective risk management helps organizations anticipate potential threats and develop proactive measures to mitigate them.

Types of Risks

Organizations face various types of risks, including:

i. Financial Risks: These include market risk, credit risk, liquidity risk, and operational risk that can impact an organization's financial health.

ii. Operational Risks: Risks arising from internal processes, systems, or human errors that can disrupt operations.

iii. Compliance and Regulatory Risks: Risks associated with failing to comply with laws, regulations, and standards, leading to penalties or legal issues.

iv. Reputational Risks: Risks that can damage an organization's reputation due to negative publicity, customer dissatisfaction, or unethical practices.

v. Strategic Risks: Risks that arise from adverse business decisions, inadequate resource allocation, or failure to respond to industry changes.

The Importance of Financial Foundations

Strong financial foundations are critical for an organization's long-term success and resilience. A solid financial base not only allows companies to absorb shocks from unexpected events but also enables them to invest in growth opportunities. Key components of financial strength include:

i. Liquidity: Having sufficient cash or liquid assets to meet short-term obligations and handle unexpected expenses.

ii. Capital Structure: Maintaining an optimal mix of debt and equity to support operations and growth without compromising financial stability.

iii. Revenue Diversification: Reducing dependence on a single source of income by expanding product lines, markets, or customer segments.

iv. Cost Management: Implementing efficient cost-control measures to enhance profitability and protect margins during downturns.

Strategies for Effective Risk Management

Implementing a robust risk management framework is essential for safeguarding organizational assets and ensuring sustainable operations. Here are several key strategies for effective risk management:

a. Risk Assessment and Analysis

Conduct regular risk assessments to identify potential threats and evaluate their likelihood and impact. This process involves:

i. Risk Identification: Identifying all possible risks relevant to the organization's operations and environment.

ii. Risk Evaluation: Analyzing the severity of each risk and its potential impact on business objectives.

iii. Prioritization: Ranking risks based on their likelihood and impact to focus resources on the most critical threats.

b. Developing a Risk Management Plan

Once risks have been identified and assessed, organizations should develop a comprehensive risk management plan that outlines:

i. Risk Mitigation Strategies: Specific actions to reduce or eliminate identified risks. This may include diversifying suppliers, investing in technology, or implementing stringent quality controls.

ii. Contingency Plans: Clear plans for responding to potential disruptions or adverse events, including communication protocols and resource allocation strategies.

iii. Monitoring and Review Processes: Establishing regular monitoring systems to track risk levels and the effectiveness of mitigation measures, with periodic reviews to update the plan as necessary.

c. Building a Risk-Aware Culture

Promoting a risk-aware culture within the organization ensures that all employees understand the importance of risk management and their role in it. Strategies for building this culture include:

i. Training and Education: Providing employees with training on risk identification, assessment, and mitigation strategies.

ii. Encouraging Open Communication: Creating channels for employees to report potential risks or concerns without fear of retribution.

iii. Incorporating Risk Management into Decision-Making: Ensuring that risk assessments are part of the strategic planning and decision-making processes at all levels of the organization.

Strengthening Financial Foundations

Building a strong financial foundation requires a multi-faceted approach, focusing on both short-term stability and long-term growth. Here are key strategies to strengthen financial resilience:

a. Effective Cash Flow Management

Maintaining healthy cash flow is critical for covering operational costs and enabling investments in growth. Strategies for effective cash flow management include:

i. Regular Cash Flow Forecasting: Anticipating cash inflows and outflows to identify potential shortfalls and plan accordingly.

ii. Optimizing Accounts Receivable: Streamlining invoicing processes, offering discounts for early payments, and implementing stringent credit controls to improve collections.

iii. Managing Inventory Levels: Keeping optimal inventory levels to reduce carrying costs while ensuring product availability.

b. Diversifying Revenue Streams

Relying on a single revenue source can be risky. Organizations should explore opportunities to diversify income by:

i. Expanding Product Lines: Introducing new products or services that complement existing offerings to attract a broader customer base.

ii. Entering New Markets: Exploring new geographic markets or customer segments to reduce dependency on existing markets.

iii. **Leveraging Strategic Partnerships:** Collaborating with other organizations to co-develop products, share resources, or access new customer bases.

c. **Investing in Technology and Innovation**

Investing in technology can enhance operational efficiency, reduce costs, and create new revenue opportunities. Organizations should prioritize:

i. **Automation:** Implementing automated systems for routine tasks to improve efficiency and reduce labor costs.

ii. **Data Analytics**: Leveraging data analytics to gain insights into customer behavior, market trends, and operational performance, enabling informed decision-making.

iii. **Continuous Improvement:** Fostering a culture of innovation that encourages employees to suggest and implement process improvements and new ideas.

Monitoring and Adapting to Changing Conditions

Both risk management and financial foundations must be continuously monitored and adapted to changing conditions. Organizations should establish key performance indicators (KPIs) to track financial health and risk exposure. Regularly reviewing these metrics allows businesses to identify emerging risks and financial weaknesses promptly.

Effectively managing risks and strengthening financial foundations are vital for businesses striving for resilience in an uncertain environment. By adopting comprehensive risk management strategies and focusing on financial stability, organizations can better navigate challenges, seize opportunities, and ensure long-term success. Building a proactive approach to risk and finance not only protects assets but also fosters a culture of resilience and adaptability, positioning companies for growth and sustainability in the face of adversity.

CHAPTER FOUR

LEVERAGING DATA ANALYTICS FOR LONG TERM SUCCESS

In the digital age, data has emerged as one of the most valuable assets for organizations seeking to achieve long-term success. The ability to harness data analytics not only empowers businesses to make informed decisions but also enhances their agility, efficiency, and competitiveness in a rapidly evolving market landscape. As organizations increasingly embrace data-driven strategies, leveraging analytics effectively becomes crucial for understanding customer behavior, predicting trends, and optimizing operations.

Understanding the Role of Data Analytics in Business Strategy

In an era marked by rapid technological advancements and an abundance of data, organizations are increasingly recognizing the pivotal role that data analytics plays in shaping effective business strategies. The ability to collect, analyze, and interpret data has transformed how businesses operate, enabling them to make informed decisions, optimize processes, and enhance customer experiences. This discussion delves into the significance of data analytics in business strategy, the various types of analytics, and how organizations can effectively integrate analytics into their strategic frameworks.

a. Informed Decision-Making

Data analytics allows businesses to make decisions based on empirical evidence rather than intuition. By analyzing historical data and current trends, organizations can identify patterns that inform strategic planning. For example, a retail company can analyze sales data to determine which products are performing well and which are underperforming, allowing for informed inventory management and targeted marketing strategies.

b. Enhanced Competitive Advantage

Businesses that effectively leverage data analytics gain a competitive edge by understanding market dynamics and customer preferences. By using data to tailor products and services to meet customer needs, companies can differentiate themselves from competitors. For instance, companies like Amazon utilize data analytics to personalize recommendations, enhancing customer satisfaction and loyalty.

c. Risk Mitigation

Data analytics is instrumental in identifying and mitigating risks. By analyzing various risk factors, organizations can anticipate challenges and implement proactive measures. For instance, financial institutions use predictive analytics to assess credit risk by examining customer data and credit histories. This allows them to make informed lending decisions and minimize potential defaults. Additionally, businesses can use data analytics to monitor operational risks and identify vulnerabilities in their supply chains, enabling them to develop contingency plans.

Key Types of Data Analytics

To fully leverage data in business strategy, organizations employ various types of analytics:

i. Descriptive Analytics

Descriptive analytics focuses on summarizing historical data to understand past performance. This type of analysis provides insights into what has happened within the organization, helping businesses identify trends and patterns. For example, a company may analyze quarterly sales data to determine which products were most successful and which required adjustments. This foundational analysis informs strategic planning and resource allocation.

ii. Diagnostic Analytics

Diagnostic analytics delves deeper into the "why" behind past outcomes. By examining historical data, organizations can identify the causes of specific events. For instance, if a company experiences a decline in sales during a particular period, diagnostic analytics can reveal underlying factors such as changes in customer preferences, pricing issues, or increased competition. Understanding these root causes enables businesses to implement targeted strategies for improvement.

iii. Predictive Analytics

Predictive analytics leverages historical data and statistical algorithms to forecast future outcomes. This type of analysis allows organizations to anticipate customer behavior and market trends. For instance, retailers can use predictive analytics to forecast demand for specific products based on past purchasing patterns, enabling them to optimize inventory levels and minimize stockouts. By anticipating changes in customer behavior, businesses can proactively adjust their strategies to align with market dynamics.

iv. Prescriptive Analytics

Prescriptive analytics goes beyond prediction by providing actionable recommendations based on data insights. This type of analysis helps organizations optimize their strategies by evaluating potential outcomes of different decisions. For example, a logistics company may use prescriptive analytics to determine the most efficient routes for deliveries, considering factors such as traffic patterns and fuel costs. By providing data-driven recommendations, organizations can enhance operational efficiency and reduce costs.

Integrating Data Analytics into Business Strategy

To effectively leverage data analytics, organizations must integrate it into their overall business strategy. Here are some key steps for successful integration:

i. Establish Clear Objectives

Organizations should define specific objectives for their data analytics initiatives. This includes identifying key questions to answer and problems to solve through data analysis. Clear objectives ensure that data efforts align with broader business goals and provide measurable outcomes.

ii. Invest in Technology and Tools

Utilizing advanced analytics tools and technologies is essential for effective data analysis. Organizations should invest in data management platforms, analytical software, and visualization tools that facilitate data collection, processing, and interpretation. The right technology stack enables businesses to extract valuable insights from their data efficiently.

iii. Foster a Data-Driven Culture

Promoting a data-driven culture is vital for encouraging the use of analytics throughout the organization. This involves training employees at all levels to understand and interpret data, fostering collaboration among departments, and creating an environment where data-driven insights are valued. A data-driven culture empowers employees to leverage analytics in their decision-making processes.

iv. Continuously Monitor and Adapt

Data analytics is an ongoing process that requires continuous monitoring of key performance indicators (KPIs) and adapting strategies based on real-time data insights. Organizations should regularly assess their data analytics efforts, measure outcomes against objectives, and refine their approaches as needed. This adaptability ensures that businesses remain agile in the face of changing market conditions.

Data analytics is a transformative force in shaping effective business strategies. By harnessing the power of data, organizations can make informed decisions, gain competitive advantages, and mitigate risks. Understanding the various types of analytics—descriptive, diagnostic, predictive, and prescriptive—enables businesses to extract valuable insights from their data. By integrating data analytics into their strategic frameworks, organizations position themselves to navigate uncertainties, seize opportunities, and drive sustainable growth in an increasingly complex business landscape. As data continues to evolve, those organizations that prioritize and effectively leverage analytics will be better equipped to thrive in the future.

Enhancing Customer Experience through Data Analytics

In the modern business landscape, where customer expectations are continually evolving, organizations are increasingly turning to data analytics to enhance customer experience (CX). The ability to collect, analyze, and interpret data from various touchpoints allows businesses to gain deep insights into customer behavior, preferences, and needs. This understanding enables companies to tailor their offerings, improve interactions, and create a more personalized experience that fosters loyalty and drives growth. This discussion explores the significance of data analytics in enhancing customer experience, the various applications of analytics in this domain, and best practices for implementation.

The Significance of Data Analytics in Customer Experience

i. Understanding Customer Behavior

Data analytics provides organizations with a comprehensive view of customer behavior. By analyzing data from multiple sources—such as website interactions, social media engagement, purchase history, and customer feedback—businesses can identify patterns and trends. Understanding how customers interact with a brand allows organizations to tailor their strategies to meet specific preferences and needs. For example, an e-commerce platform can analyze user behavior to determine which products are frequently viewed together, enabling them to recommend complementary items during the shopping process.

ii. Personalization and Targeted Marketing

One of the most powerful applications of data analytics in enhancing customer experience is personalization. By leveraging insights from data, organizations can create targeted marketing campaigns that resonate with individual customers. For instance, retailers can use past purchase data to send personalized recommendations via email or push notifications, increasing the likelihood of repeat purchases. This level of personalization enhances the customer experience, as customers feel understood and valued by the brand.

iii. Anticipating Customer Needs

Predictive analytics plays a crucial role in anticipating customer needs and preferences. By analyzing historical data, businesses can forecast future behaviors, allowing them to proactively address customer expectations. For example, a subscription service can analyze user data to predict when a customer is likely to renew their subscription or upgrade their plan. By sending timely reminders or offers, businesses can enhance customer satisfaction and retention.

iv. Improving Customer Support

Data analytics can also enhance customer support by providing insights into common customer issues and concerns. By analyzing customer interactions across various channels, organizations can identify trends in inquiries or complaints. This allows businesses to streamline their support processes and implement proactive measures. For example, if data reveals a common issue with a product, a company can address it through improved FAQs, tutorials, or product modifications, thereby enhancing the overall customer experience.

Applications of Data Analytics in Customer Experience

Organizations can leverage data analytics in several key areas to enhance customer experience:

i. Customer Segmentation

Data analytics enables businesses to segment their customers based on various attributes such as demographics, purchasing behavior, and preferences. This segmentation allows organizations to tailor their marketing efforts and product offerings to meet the specific needs of different customer groups. For instance, a travel company may segment customers based on their travel preferences—adventure seekers, luxury travelers, or family vacationers—and create targeted marketing campaigns for each segment.

ii. Journey Mapping

Understanding the customer journey is essential for enhancing customer experience. Data analytics can help businesses map out the various touchpoints customers encounter when interacting with a brand. By analyzing customer interactions across these touchpoints, organizations can identify pain points and areas for improvement. For example, if data reveals that customers frequently abandon their shopping carts, businesses can investigate the reasons behind this behavior and implement changes to reduce friction in the checkout process.

iii. Sentiment Analysis

Sentiment analysis involves using natural language processing (NLP) to analyze customer feedback and sentiment expressed through various channels, including social media, reviews, and surveys. By understanding how customers feel about their products or services, organizations can gain valuable insights into areas of improvement. For example, if sentiment analysis reveals negative feedback about a specific product feature, businesses can prioritize changes to enhance customer satisfaction.

iv. Performance Metrics and KPIs

Data analytics allows organizations to track key performance indicators (KPIs) related to customer experience. Metrics such as Net Promoter Score (NPS), Customer Satisfaction Score (CSAT), and Customer Effort Score (CES) provide valuable insights into how customers perceive their interactions with a brand. By continuously monitoring these metrics, organizations can assess the effectiveness of their customer experience initiatives and make data-driven adjustments.

Best Practices for Implementing Data Analytics in Customer Experience

To successfully leverage data analytics for enhancing customer experience, organizations should consider the following best practices:

i. Establish Clear Objectives

Before implementing data analytics initiatives, organizations should define clear objectives related to customer experience. This includes identifying specific questions to answer, problems to address, and desired outcomes. Clear objectives ensure that data efforts align with overall business goals and provide measurable results.

ii. Invest in the Right Technology

Utilizing advanced analytics tools and technologies is crucial for effective data analysis. Organizations should invest in customer relationship management (CRM) systems, data visualization tools, and analytics platforms that facilitate data collection, processing, and interpretation. The right technology stack enables businesses to extract valuable insights from their customer data efficiently.

iii. Foster a Data-Driven Culture

Creating a data-driven culture is vital for encouraging the use of analytics across the organization. This involves training employees at all levels to understand and interpret data, fostering collaboration among departments, and promoting an environment where data-driven insights are valued. A data-driven culture empowers employees to leverage analytics in their decision-making processes.

iv. Continuously Monitor and Adapt

Data analytics is an ongoing process that requires continuous monitoring and adaptation. Organizations should regularly assess their customer experience initiatives, measure outcomes against objectives, and refine their approaches based on real-time data insights. This adaptability ensures that businesses remain responsive to changing customer needs and preferences.

Enhancing customer experience through data analytics is no longer a luxury but a necessity for organizations seeking to thrive in a competitive landscape. By leveraging data to understand customer behavior, personalize offerings, anticipate needs, and improve support, businesses can create a more satisfying and engaging experience for their customers. Through effective segmentation, journey mapping, sentiment analysis, and performance tracking, organizations can continuously refine their strategies and drive long-term customer loyalty. As data analytics continues to evolve, businesses that prioritize its integration into their customer experience initiatives will be better positioned to meet and exceed customer expectations, ultimately leading to sustained growth and success.

CHAPTER FIVE

FINANCIAL PLANNING FOR SCALABLE AND RESILIENT BUSINESS

In an increasingly competitive and dynamic business environment, scalability is essential for long-term success. A scalable business model allows a company to grow its revenue without a corresponding increase in costs, enabling it to adapt to market demands efficiently. At the heart of this scalability lies a robust financial model that provides a framework for understanding the financial implications of growth and guiding strategic decisions.

The Importance of Financial Models for Scalability

i. Strategic Decision-Making

Financial models serve as powerful tools for strategic decision-making. They provide a quantitative basis for evaluating various growth scenarios and their potential impact on the organization's financial health. By simulating different situations, such as market expansions, product launches, or changes in pricing strategy, businesses can assess the financial feasibility of these initiatives and make informed choices.

ii. Resource Allocation

As businesses scale, efficient resource allocation becomes critical. Financial models help organizations prioritize investments by identifying the most promising opportunities. For example, a company may use a financial model to evaluate the potential return on investment (ROI) for launching a new product versus expanding its existing offerings. This analysis ensures that resources are directed toward initiatives with the highest potential for growth and profitability.

iii. Performance Measurement

Financial models provide a framework for measuring and tracking performance against predefined goals. By establishing key performance indicators (KPIs) and integrating them into the financial model, organizations can monitor their progress and make necessary adjustments. This continuous feedback loop allows businesses to stay on course toward their scalability objectives.

Types of Financial Models for Scalability

Several financial models can support scalability, each with its unique features and applications:

i. Revenue Model

The revenue model outlines how a business generates income. It includes various streams, such as product sales, subscriptions, licensing fees, or service charges. Understanding the revenue model is essential for scalability, as it helps businesses identify opportunities to expand revenue streams. For instance, a software company might transition from a one-time purchase model to a subscription-based model, creating a more predictable and scalable revenue stream.

ii. Cost Structure Model

The cost structure model categorizes the expenses associated with running the business. It distinguishes between fixed and variable costs, providing insight into how costs behave as the business scales. A scalable business should aim to minimize fixed costs relative to variable costs, allowing for greater flexibility in responding to market changes. For example, a company that relies heavily on fixed assets may struggle to scale effectively, while a business with a predominantly variable cost structure can adapt more easily to fluctuations in demand.

iii. Profitability Model

The profitability model analyzes the relationship between revenue and costs to determine the business's overall profitability. This model helps organizations assess their margins and identify areas for improvement. By focusing on enhancing profitability, businesses can create a solid foundation for scaling. For instance, a company might identify cost-saving opportunities in its supply chain to improve its gross margin, making it easier to fund future growth initiatives.

iv. Cash Flow Model

A cash flow model tracks the inflow and outflow of cash over time, providing insights into the company's liquidity position. Maintaining healthy cash flow is vital for scaling, as it ensures that the business can meet its operational obligations and invest in growth opportunities. By projecting future cash flows, businesses can anticipate potential shortfalls and take proactive measures, such as securing additional financing or adjusting spending, to ensure stability.

v. Scenario Analysis Model

Scenario analysis involves creating different financial projections based on various assumptions about the future. This model allows businesses to explore best-case, worst-case, and most-likely scenarios, providing a comprehensive understanding of potential risks and rewards. By preparing for different outcomes, organizations can develop contingency plans and adapt their strategies to changing market conditions. For instance, a company might analyze the financial implications of entering a new market during economic uncertainty versus a stable economic environment.

Implementing Financial Models for Scalability

To effectively implement financial models for scalability, businesses should consider the following steps:

i. Define Clear Objectives

Organizations should begin by defining clear scalability objectives. This involves identifying the specific growth targets they wish to achieve, such as increasing revenue by a certain percentage or expanding into new markets. Clear objectives provide a framework for developing and refining financial models.

ii. Gather Accurate Data

Reliable data is the foundation of effective financial modeling. Businesses should ensure they have access to accurate historical data, including sales figures, expense reports, and market research. This data will inform the assumptions used in the financial models and enhance their reliability.

iii. Choose the Right Modeling Tools

Selecting the appropriate financial modeling tools is crucial for effective implementation. Many software options are available, ranging from basic spreadsheet applications to sophisticated financial modeling software. Organizations should choose tools that align with their complexity needs and user expertise.

iv. Involve Key Stakeholders

Engaging key stakeholders in the modeling process ensures that various perspectives are considered. Involving finance teams, marketing professionals, and operational leaders can provide valuable insights and enhance the accuracy of the models. Collaboration fosters buy-in and commitment to the growth strategy.

v. Regularly Update and Review Models

Financial models should not be static; they require regular updates and reviews to reflect changing market conditions and business circumstances. Organizations should establish a schedule for revisiting their models, incorporating new data, and adjusting assumptions as necessary.

Understanding financial models for scalability is essential for businesses seeking to navigate growth effectively in an increasingly competitive landscape. By leveraging these models, organizations can make informed decisions, allocate resources efficiently, and measure performance against their scalability objectives. Various financial models, including revenue, cost structure, profitability, cash flow, and scenario analysis models, provide valuable insights into the financial implications of growth. By implementing these models thoughtfully and collaboratively, businesses can position themselves for sustainable growth and long-term success in an ever-evolving market.

Budgeting for Growth: Short-Term vs. Long-Term Planning

Successful budgeting is fundamental to a company's growth trajectory. As organizations strive to expand, balancing short-term operational needs with long-term strategic goals becomes increasingly complex. Understanding the distinction between short-term and long-term

budgeting is essential for aligning financial resources with the company's growth objectives. This discussion explores the importance of both short-term and long-term budgeting, how they differ, and strategies for effectively managing both to drive sustainable growth.

The Importance of Budgeting for Growth

Budgeting plays a crucial role in enabling businesses to plan for future growth while maintaining financial health. Proper budgeting allows organizations to allocate resources effectively, anticipate cash flow needs, and make informed investment decisions. An effective budgeting strategy provides a roadmap for achieving growth targets, minimizing financial risks, and ensuring that the organization can adapt to changing market conditions.

Short-Term Budgeting

Short-term budgeting typically covers a one-year period and focuses on immediate operational needs. It emphasizes cash flow management, day-to-day expenses, and short-term revenue generation. Key components of short-term budgeting include:

i. Operational Efficiency

Short-term budgets help businesses optimize their operational efficiency by providing a clear view of monthly or quarterly expenses. By closely monitoring these costs, organizations can identify areas for cost savings and ensure that they are using their resources efficiently. This efficiency is vital for maintaining profitability while pursuing growth initiatives.

ii. Cash Flow Management

A critical aspect of short-term budgeting is ensuring that the organization has sufficient cash flow to meet its obligations. This involves projecting cash inflows and outflows, identifying potential cash shortages, and developing strategies to address them. Effective cash flow management allows businesses to respond quickly to unexpected challenges, such as fluctuating demand or rising costs.

iii. Performance Monitoring

Short-term budgets serve as benchmarks for evaluating financial performance. By comparing actual results to budgeted figures, organizations can assess how well they are executing their operational plans. This performance monitoring enables businesses to make timely adjustments, such as reallocating resources or revising strategies, to stay on track toward their growth objectives.

Long-Term Budgeting

Long-term budgeting typically spans a period of three to five years and focuses on strategic growth initiatives. This type of budgeting emphasizes investments in areas that will drive future growth, such as new product development, market expansion, and infrastructure improvements. Key components of long-term budgeting include:

i. Strategic Vision

Long-term budgeting aligns financial resources with the organization's strategic vision. It involves identifying growth opportunities, setting ambitious but achievable goals, and developing a roadmap for reaching those goals. This alignment ensures that investments are directed toward initiatives that will yield significant returns over time.

ii. Capital Investment Planning

Long-term budgets facilitate capital investment planning by outlining the funding required for major projects. This may include investments in technology, facilities, or workforce expansion. By anticipating future capital needs, businesses can secure financing, negotiate favorable terms, and plan for the financial implications of their growth strategies.

iii. Risk Management

Long-term budgeting incorporates risk assessment and management strategies. Businesses must consider various external factors, such as economic fluctuations, regulatory changes, and market competition, that could impact their growth plans. By integrating risk management into the budgeting process, organizations can develop contingency plans and make informed decisions to mitigate potential setbacks.

Balancing Short-Term and Long-Term Budgeting

Achieving growth requires a careful balance between short-term and long-term budgeting. Here are some strategies to effectively manage both:

i. Integrate Budgets

Organizations should integrate short-term and long-term budgets to create a cohesive financial strategy. This involves ensuring that short-term budgets support long-term growth objectives while also allowing for flexibility to adapt to changing circumstances.

ii. Set Clear Priorities

Establishing clear priorities helps businesses allocate resources effectively between short-term and long-term initiatives. Organizations should identify which projects or expenses are critical to immediate success and which investments will drive future growth.

iii. Conduct Regular Reviews

Regularly reviewing both short-term and long-term budgets allows businesses to assess their progress and make necessary adjustments. These reviews should consider changing market conditions, shifts in consumer behavior, and internal performance metrics.

iv. Engage Stakeholders

Involving key stakeholders in the budgeting process fosters collaboration and ensures that different perspectives are considered. This engagement can lead to better-informed decision-making and alignment on growth objectives.

v. Embrace Flexibility

The business landscape is constantly evolving, and organizations must remain agile in their budgeting approaches. Incorporating flexibility into both short-term and long-term budgets enables businesses to adapt quickly to new opportunities or challenges.

Effective budgeting is crucial for driving growth and ensuring long-term sustainability. By understanding the differences between short-term and long-term budgeting, organizations can align their financial resources with their strategic objectives. Short-term budgeting focuses on operational efficiency and cash flow management, while long-term budgeting emphasizes strategic vision and capital investment planning. Balancing both types of budgeting enable businesses to navigate growth challenges and seize opportunities in an ever-changing market landscape. Through thoughtful integration, clear prioritization, and regular reviews, organizations can position themselves for success and achieve their growth ambitions.

Risk Management in Financial Planning

Effective financial planning is integral to the success of any organization. However, with potential rewards come inherent risks that can threaten the stability and longevity of a business. Risk management within financial planning involves identifying, assessing, and mitigating risks to ensure that an organization can achieve its financial objectives. This discussion explores the significance of risk management in financial planning, key components of an effective risk management strategy, and best practices for integrating risk management into the financial planning process.

The Importance of Risk Management in Financial Planning

i. Protecting Assets and Investments

One of the primary roles of risk management in financial planning is to safeguard an organization's assets and investments. By identifying potential risks—such as market fluctuations, regulatory changes, or operational disruptions—businesses can take proactive measures to protect their financial resources. This protective approach is essential for maintaining financial stability and ensuring that the organization can continue to operate effectively.

ii. Enhancing Decision-Making

Informed decision-making is a critical aspect of successful financial planning. Risk management provides valuable insights that enable organizations to make sound financial decisions. By understanding potential risks and their implications, businesses can weigh the benefits and drawbacks of various financial strategies, leading to more informed choices that align with their objectives.

iii. Ensuring Compliance and Governance

Compliance with regulations and governance standards is essential for maintaining the trust of stakeholders, including investors, customers, and regulatory bodies. A comprehensive risk management strategy helps organizations identify compliance-related risks and implement controls to mitigate them. This not only protects the organization from legal issues and penalties but also fosters a culture of accountability and transparency.

iv. Improving Financial Performance

Effective risk management contributes to improved financial performance. By proactively addressing risks, organizations can minimize potential losses and capitalize on opportunities that arise from changing market conditions. This proactive approach leads to better resource allocation, more strategic investments, and ultimately, enhanced profitability.

Key Components of Risk Management in Financial Planning

i. Risk Identification

The first step in risk management is identifying potential risks that could impact the organization's financial health. This includes both internal risks—such as operational inefficiencies, financial mismanagement, and cybersecurity threats—and external risks, such as market volatility, economic downturns, and changes in consumer behavior. Tools such as risk assessments, scenario analysis, and brainstorming sessions can help organizations identify and categorize risks effectively.

ii. Risk Assessment

Once risks have been identified, organizations must assess their potential impact and likelihood of occurrence. This involves evaluating the severity of each risk and determining how it could affect the organization's financial performance. Risk assessment typically involves quantitative methods, such as financial modeling and statistical analysis, as well as qualitative methods, such as expert judgment and stakeholder input.

iii. Risk Mitigation

Risk mitigation involves developing strategies to reduce or eliminate identified risks. This may include implementing risk controls, such as diversifying investments, securing insurance, or establishing contingency plans. Additionally, organizations can adopt risk transfer strategies, such as outsourcing certain functions or entering into partnerships that share risks. The goal of risk mitigation is to minimize the potential negative impact of risks on the organization's financial objectives.

iv. Monitoring and Reporting

Ongoing monitoring of risks is essential to ensure that risk management strategies remain effective. Organizations should establish key performance indicators (KPIs) to track risk exposure and the effectiveness of mitigation measures. Regular reporting on risk management activities helps keep stakeholders informed and ensures that risk management remains a priority within the organization.

v. Continuous Improvement

Risk management is an iterative process that requires continuous improvement. Organizations should regularly review and update their risk management strategies to reflect changes in the business environment, emerging risks, and lessons learned from past experiences. This commitment to continuous improvement fosters a proactive risk management culture and enhances the organization's resilience.

Best Practices for Integrating Risk Management into Financial Planning

i. Establish a Risk Management Framework

Creating a formal risk management framework is essential for integrating risk management into financial planning. This framework should outline roles and responsibilities, risk assessment processes, and risk reporting procedures.

Establishing a clear framework ensures that risk management is embedded in the organizational culture and decision-making processes.

ii. Engage Stakeholders

Involving key stakeholders in the risk management process fosters collaboration and ensures that various perspectives are considered. Engaging stakeholders, including finance teams, operational leaders, and external advisors, enhances the effectiveness of risk management strategies and helps align them with the organization's overall objectives.

iii. Leverage Technology

Utilizing technology can enhance risk management efforts by automating data collection, analysis, and reporting. Advanced analytics and data visualization tools can help organizations gain insights into risk exposure and make informed decisions. Additionally, technology can facilitate scenario modeling and stress testing, allowing businesses to evaluate the potential impact of various risks on their financial plans.

iv. Provide Training and Education

Training employees on risk management practices is essential for fostering a risk-aware culture. Organizations should invest in training programs that educate employees about identifying, assessing, and mitigating risks. This knowledge equips employees to make informed decisions and contributes to a collective commitment to managing risks effectively.

v. Communicate Transparently

Clear and transparent communication regarding risk management initiatives is vital for building trust among stakeholders. Organizations should regularly share information about their risk management strategies, progress, and challenges. This transparency not only fosters accountability but also encourages a culture of open dialogue around risk management.

Risk management is an integral component of effective financial planning. By identifying, assessing, and mitigating risks, organizations can protect their assets, enhance decision-making, ensure compliance, and improve financial performance. A comprehensive risk management strategy involves several key components, including risk identification, assessment, mitigation, monitoring, and continuous improvement. By adopting best practices such as establishing a risk management framework, engaging stakeholders, leveraging technology, providing training, and communicating transparently, organizations can successfully integrate risk management into their financial planning processes. This proactive approach not only supports financial stability but also positions businesses for sustainable growth in an increasingly complex and uncertain environment.

CHAPTER SIX

INNOVATION AS A CORE DRIVER OF BUSINESS SUSTAINABILITY

In an era marked by rapid environmental changes, shifting consumer preferences, and increasing regulatory pressures, businesses face the imperative of not only achieving profitability but also ensuring long-term sustainability. Innovation emerges as a crucial driver in this context, enabling organizations to adapt, thrive, and contribute positively to society and the environment. By integrating innovative practices into their operations, companies can foster sustainability, enhance competitiveness, and create value for stakeholders.

The Importance of Innovation in Business Sustainability

i. Enhancing Resource Efficiency

Innovation plays a pivotal role in improving resource efficiency, which is essential for sustainability. Through the development of new processes, technologies, and materials, businesses can reduce waste, lower energy consumption, and optimize the use of raw materials. For instance, companies that invest in innovative manufacturing techniques often find ways to minimize scrap, recycle materials, and enhance energy efficiency, thereby reducing their environmental footprint.

ii. Creating Sustainable Products and Services

Sustainable innovation enables businesses to design products and services that meet the evolving needs of consumers while minimizing environmental impact. This includes creating eco-friendly products, utilizing sustainable materials, and implementing circular economy principles, where products are designed for reuse, refurbishment, or recycling. By offering sustainable options, companies can attract environmentally conscious consumers and differentiate themselves in the market.

iii. Meeting Regulatory and Market Demands

As governments and regulatory bodies increasingly emphasize sustainability, businesses must innovate to comply with new standards and expectations. Innovation allows organizations to proactively address regulatory challenges, reduce compliance costs, and enhance their reputations. Moreover, as consumers demand greater transparency and sustainability from brands, innovative practices can help companies build trust and loyalty among their customer base.

iv. Driving Economic Growth and Competitiveness

Investing in innovation not only contributes to sustainability but also drives economic growth. Innovative businesses are often more resilient, adaptable, and capable of navigating market changes. By fostering a culture of innovation, companies can stimulate economic activity, create jobs, and contribute to a thriving economy while maintaining a commitment to sustainable practices.

Integrating Sustainability into the Innovation Process

To harness the full potential of innovation as a driver of sustainability, organizations must integrate sustainability principles throughout the innovation process. This involves:

i. Adopting a Systems Thinking Approach

A systems thinking approach encourages businesses to view innovation within the broader context of their operations, supply chains, and the environment. By understanding the interconnectedness of various components, organizations can identify opportunities for innovation that promote sustainability across multiple dimensions.

ii. Engaging Stakeholders

Collaboration with stakeholders including employees, customers, suppliers, and community members—is crucial for successful sustainable innovation. Engaging diverse perspectives can lead to the development of creative solutions that address sustainability challenges while meeting market demands.

iii. Investing in Research and Development

Investment in research and development (R&D) is essential for driving sustainable innovation. Organizations that prioritize R&D can explore new technologies, materials, and processes that align with sustainability goals. This commitment to innovation can lead to breakthroughs that enhance both environmental performance and business outcomes.

iv. Implementing Agile Methodologies

Adopting agile methodologies in the innovation process allows organizations to respond quickly to changing market conditions and consumer preferences. This flexibility enables businesses to experiment with new ideas, iterate on designs, and refine products in a way that prioritizes sustainability.

Case Studies of Successful Sustainable Innovations

Real-world examples illustrate how innovation can drive business sustainability effectively:

i. Unilever: Sustainable Living Plan

Unilever's Sustainable Living Plan outlines its commitment to reducing its environmental impact while increasing social benefits. The company has implemented innovative practices, such as developing biodegradable packaging and promoting sustainable sourcing of raw materials. This approach has allowed Unilever to enhance its brand reputation and attract environmentally conscious consumers.

ii. Tesla: Revolutionizing Electric Vehicles

Tesla has disrupted the automotive industry by pioneering electric vehicles (EVs) and energy storage solutions. Through continuous innovation in battery technology and sustainable energy solutions, Tesla has not only contributed to reducing greenhouse gas emissions but has also positioned itself as a leader in the transition to a sustainable energy future.

iii. Patagonia: Circular Economy Initiatives

Patagonia has integrated sustainability into its business model through initiatives focused on circular economy principles. The company encourages customers to repair and recycle their products and offers programs like Worn Wear, which allows customers to buy and sell used Patagonia gear. This innovative approach promotes sustainability while enhancing customer loyalty.

Measuring the Impact of Innovation on Sustainability Goals

To ensure that innovation contributes effectively to sustainability objectives, businesses must implement methods for measuring its impact. Key performance indicators (KPIs) can help organizations track progress and assess the effectiveness of their sustainable innovation initiatives. Common metrics include:

i. Reduction in Carbon Footprint: Measuring greenhouse gas emissions before and after implementing sustainable innovations provides insight into the environmental impact.

ii. Resource Efficiency Gains: Tracking changes in resource usage, such as water and energy consumption, helps organizations understand the efficiency improvements resulting from innovative practices.

iii. Customer Engagement and Satisfaction: Assessing consumer feedback and engagement levels related to sustainable products can indicate the success of innovation efforts in meeting market demands.

Challenges and Opportunities in Driving Sustainable Innovation

Despite the benefits of integrating innovation and sustainability, organizations often face challenges, including:

i. Resource Constraints: Limited financial and human resources can hinder investment in sustainable innovation initiatives. Companies must find ways to allocate resources effectively while prioritizing sustainability.

ii. Cultural Resistance: Changing organizational culture to prioritize sustainability can be challenging. Leaders must foster a culture of innovation that encourages experimentation and embraces sustainable practices.

iii. Market Uncertainty: Rapidly changing market conditions can create uncertainty around the feasibility and profitability of sustainable innovations. Organizations need to remain agile and adaptable in the face of these changes.

Conversely, numerous opportunities exist for businesses to leverage innovation as a core driver of sustainability:

i. Technological Advancements: Emerging technologies, such as artificial intelligence, blockchain, and renewable energy solutions, present opportunities for organizations to enhance sustainability through innovative applications.

ii. Collaborative Ecosystems: Partnerships with other businesses, non-profits, and research institutions can drive collective innovation efforts toward sustainability goals, leading to shared benefits and greater impact.

iii. Consumer Demand for Sustainability: As consumers increasingly prioritize sustainability in their purchasing decisions, businesses can capitalize on this trend by innovating to meet these preferences and differentiate themselves in the marketplace.

Innovation is an essential driver of business sustainability, enabling organizations to enhance resource efficiency, create sustainable products, comply with regulations, and improve overall financial performance. By integrating sustainability principles into the innovation process, businesses can unlock new opportunities, address challenges, and build resilience in an ever-evolving market landscape. Through case studies, measurement strategies, and a focus on overcoming challenges, organizations can effectively leverage innovation as a core component of their sustainability strategies, positioning themselves for long-term success in a rapidly changing world.

Case Studies of Successful Sustainable Innovations

Sustainable innovation is crucial for businesses looking to address environmental challenges, meet regulatory requirements, and respond to changing consumer preferences. Many companies have embraced this challenge, developing groundbreaking innovations that drive both sustainability and business growth. These case studies highlight organizations that have successfully integrated sustainability into their operations through innovative practices, setting an example for others to follow.

Unilever's Sustainable Living Plan

Unilever, a global leader in consumer goods, is renowned for its commitment to sustainability through the Sustainable Living Plan. The company set ambitious goals to reduce its environmental impact while improving social outcomes. Through innovative approaches, Unilever aims to decouple growth from its environmental footprint and increase positive social impacts by addressing issues such as health, hygiene, and fair trade.

Key innovations from Unilever include:

Eco-friendly Packaging: Unilever has introduced biodegradable and recyclable packaging solutions to reduce plastic waste. By replacing conventional plastics with plant-based materials and designing packaging for circularity, Unilever has significantly reduced its reliance on virgin plastics.

Sustainable Sourcing: The company focuses on sourcing 100% of its agricultural raw materials sustainably. For example, it has implemented innovative sourcing methods in its supply chains, including sustainable palm oil and tea production practices.

Water and Energy Efficiency: Unilever has also pioneered energy-efficient manufacturing technologies and water-saving initiatives in its factories, aiming to halve the environmental impact of its operations.

Through these innovations, Unilever has reduced its carbon footprint and plastic waste while driving profitability. The company's sustainable practices have not only attracted environmentally conscious consumers but have also earned recognition from stakeholders and increased customer loyalty.

Tesla's Electric Vehicles and Energy Solutions

Tesla is an iconic example of innovation that has redefined an entire industry while focusing on sustainability. Tesla's mission "to accelerate the world's transition to sustainable energy" drives its focus on electric vehicles (EVs), solar energy, and energy storage solutions. By constantly pushing the boundaries of technology, Tesla has made significant contributions to reducing global reliance on fossil fuels.

Tesla's key sustainable innovations include:

Electric Vehicles (EVs): Tesla revolutionized the automotive industry by making electric vehicles mainstream. Its EVs, such as the Model S, Model 3, and Model Y, are powered by cutting-edge battery technology and produce zero emissions, offering a sustainable alternative to gasoline-powered cars. By scaling production and improving battery range, Tesla has made EVs accessible to a wider audience.

Battery Technology: Tesla's innovations in battery technology have been crucial to the success of its EVs. Its Gigafactories, which produce lithium-ion batteries on a massive scale, have enabled Tesla to reduce costs and increase energy storage efficiency, driving the broader adoption of clean energy.

Renewable Energy Solutions: Tesla's solar energy products, including solar panels and Solar Roofs, allow homeowners and businesses to generate their own clean energy. Tesla's Powerwall, a home battery system, enables users to store renewable energy for use during outages or peak demand times, promoting energy independence.

Tesla's innovative products have not only reduced the carbon footprint of transportation and energy consumption but have also positioned the company as a leader in the global transition to renewable energy. Tesla's market success has proven that sustainability and profitability can go hand in hand.

Patagonia's Circular Economy Initiatives

Outdoor apparel company Patagonia is widely regarded as a pioneer in sustainable business practices. The company's commitment to environmental responsibility has led to numerous innovations aimed at reducing waste, encouraging reuse, and promoting sustainable production.

Key sustainable innovations from Patagonia include:

Worn Wear Program: Patagonia launched the Worn Wear program to encourage customers to buy, sell, and trade used Patagonia products. The program promotes the reuse of garments and reduces the need for new production, aligning with the principles of the circular economy. Patagonia also offers repairs on damaged products to extend their lifespan.

Recycled Materials: Patagonia has made significant investments in the use of recycled materials in its products. The company's iconic fleece jackets are made from recycled plastic bottles, and it continues to innovate in sourcing materials that reduce environmental impact. For example, Patagonia uses organic cotton, recycled polyester, and responsibly sourced wool.

Environmental Activism and Advocacy: Beyond its products, Patagonia has taken a leadership role in advocating for environmental protection. The company donates 1% of its sales to environmental causes and has supported grassroots organizations working to address climate change and protect public lands.

By embracing sustainable innovation, Patagonia has built a loyal customer base and enhanced its brand reputation. The company's focus on environmental stewardship, combined with its commitment to quality, has driven long-term success while staying true to its mission of preserving the planet.

IKEA's Renewable Energy Commitment

IKEA, the world's largest furniture retailer, has made sustainability central to its business strategy, with a focus on reducing its carbon footprint and promoting renewable energy. Through innovation in its supply chain, product design, and energy use, IKEA is working to become a circular and climate-positive business by 2030.

Key innovations from IKEA include:

Renewable Energy Investments: IKEA has invested heavily in renewable energy, with a commitment to produce more renewable energy than it consumes by 2030. The company has installed solar panels on many of its stores and warehouses, and it has invested in wind farms globally to generate clean energy.

Sustainable Product Design: IKEA is committed to creating products that are more sustainable throughout their life cycles. The company uses sustainable materials, such as FSC-certified wood and recycled plastics, in its furniture. Additionally, IKEA designs products with a focus on modularity, encouraging consumers to repair or upgrade items rather than discard them.

Energy-Efficient Products: IKEA's product offerings include energy-efficient solutions, such as LED lighting, which helps consumers reduce their energy consumption at home. The company has also developed sustainable home products, such as water-saving faucets and solar-powered lamps, that empower customers to live more sustainably.

IKEA's sustainable innovations have not only reduced its environmental impact but also created long-term value for the company and its customers. By aligning its business strategy with sustainability goals, IKEA has demonstrated how innovation can drive both environmental and economic success.

Nike's Sustainable Product Innovation

Nike, one of the world's leading sportswear brands, has integrated sustainability into its product innovation process, focusing on reducing waste and lowering the environmental impact of its manufacturing operations. Through initiatives like Nike's Move to Zero campaign, the company is working to achieve zero carbon and zero waste across its value chain.

Key innovations from Nike include:

Nike Flyknit Technology: Nike developed Flyknit, a manufacturing technology that reduces material waste by knitting shoes from a single strand of yarn. Flyknit shoes are lighter, use fewer materials, and generate less waste during production. This innovation has significantly reduced Nike's environmental footprint while offering high-performance products to athletes.

Sustainable Materials: Nike has committed to using more sustainable materials in its products. For example, Nike Air soles are made from at least 50% recycled materials, and the company is developing new sustainable fabrics, such as recycled polyester and organic cotton, for its apparel lines.

Circular Design: Nike is exploring circular design principles, encouraging the recycling and reuse of its products. The company's Nike Grind initiative repurposes old shoes and manufacturing scraps into new materials for sports surfaces, playgrounds, and new Nike products.

Nike's focus on sustainable innovation has allowed the company to remain a leader in the competitive sportswear market while reducing its environmental impact. The brand's commitment to sustainability resonates with eco-conscious consumers, further strengthening its global presence.

These case studies illustrate how businesses across various industries have successfully integrated sustainable innovation into their operations. Whether through eco-friendly product design, circular economy initiatives, or investments in renewable energy, these companies demonstrate that innovation is essential to achieving long-term sustainability. By embracing sustainability as a core value, businesses not only reduce their environmental impact but also drive profitability, enhance brand reputation, and secure a competitive advantage in the market.

Challenges and Opportunities in Driving Sustainable Innovation

Sustainable innovation has become a key focus for businesses seeking to balance growth with environmental and social responsibility. However, the road to achieving sustainability-driven innovation is filled with both challenges and opportunities. While companies that successfully integrate sustainability into their operations can reap numerous benefits—such as enhanced brand reputation, customer loyalty, and long-term profitability—there are hurdles to overcome. This analysis delves into the key challenges businesses face in pursuing sustainable innovation and highlights the opportunities that can arise from embracing sustainability.

Challenges in Driving Sustainable Innovation

a. High Initial Costs and Investment

One of the most significant challenges in driving sustainable innovation is the high upfront cost associated with research, development, and implementation of sustainable practices. Many eco-friendly technologies, renewable energy systems, and sustainable manufacturing processes require substantial capital investment. Small and medium-sized enterprises (SMEs) in particular may struggle with securing the necessary funds to pursue these innovations, as they often lack access to large pools of capital or government incentives that larger corporations can tap into.

Additionally, sustainable materials and production methods can be more expensive than their traditional counterparts, making it challenging for companies to balance cost-efficiency with environmental goals in the short term.

b. Resistance to Change and Organizational Inertia

Another major challenge is the cultural resistance to change within organizations. Sustainable innovation often requires rethinking existing business models, redesigning products, or altering long-established operational processes. Employees and stakeholders may be resistant to adopting new practices, particularly if they feel that sustainable approaches are more complex, time-consuming, or risky. Overcoming this inertia requires effective leadership, clear communication, and a commitment to sustainability from the top down.

Changing consumer behavior is also a significant obstacle. Despite growing awareness of environmental issues, not all customers are willing to pay a premium for sustainable products, especially in price-sensitive markets. Businesses must strike a delicate balance between offering eco-friendly products and maintaining competitive pricing.

c. Regulatory and Compliance Complexities

The rapidly evolving regulatory landscape related to environmental protection and sustainability presents both a challenge and an opportunity. Many governments have implemented stringent regulations aimed at reducing carbon emissions, waste, and resource consumption. Navigating these regulations can be complex, particularly for companies operating in multiple jurisdictions with different rules and compliance requirements.

Additionally, businesses must stay ahead of future regulatory changes that may mandate stricter sustainability standards. Adopting sustainable innovation early can help companies avoid potential fines or operational disruptions, but it requires constant vigilance and flexibility.

d. Supply Chain Constraints

Sustainable innovation often requires rethinking supply chains, from sourcing raw materials to manufacturing processes and distribution. Finding suppliers that adhere to ethical and sustainable practices can be difficult, especially in industries with long, complex supply chains. Businesses that source materials from developing regions may face challenges ensuring that their suppliers meet environmental and labor standards.

Moreover, disruptions in the global supply chain, such as those caused by geopolitical tensions or natural disasters, can further complicate the adoption of sustainable practices. Businesses must carefully vet their suppliers and consider localizing or diversifying their supply chains to mitigate these risks.

Opportunities in Driving Sustainable Innovation

a. Competitive Differentiation and Brand Loyalty

One of the most significant opportunities in sustainable innovation is the ability to differentiate a brand in an increasingly competitive marketplace. Consumers are becoming more environmentally conscious and are actively seeking out companies that align with their values. Brands that are able to demonstrate a genuine commitment to sustainability—through transparent supply chains, eco-friendly products, or carbon-neutral operations—can build stronger connections with customers and foster long-term loyalty.

Sustainability can also be a powerful marketing tool. Companies that showcase their innovative efforts in sustainability can attract a growing segment of consumers who prioritize ethical consumption and environmental responsibility. Additionally, brands that are known for their sustainable practices often enjoy enhanced reputation and goodwill, particularly among younger, socially conscious consumers.

b. Long-Term Cost Savings

While sustainable innovation may require significant upfront investment, it can lead to substantial cost savings in the long run. Energy-efficient technologies, waste reduction initiatives, and optimized supply chains often reduce operating costs over time. For example, companies that invest in renewable energy solutions, such as solar or wind power, can lower their energy bills and reduce their reliance on fossil fuels.

In addition, companies that implement circular economy principles—such as recycling, reusing, and repurposing materials—can cut down on raw material costs and reduce waste management expenses. These cost savings can enhance profitability and resilience, making sustainable innovation a sound financial investment for the future.

c. Access to New Markets and Business Models

Sustainable innovation opens up opportunities for businesses to enter new markets or create entirely new business models. For example, the increasing demand for electric vehicles, renewable energy, and sustainable fashion has given rise to new industries and growth opportunities for businesses that prioritize sustainability.

Additionally, adopting sustainable practices can enable businesses to participate in new ecosystems, such as the circular economy or carbon trading markets. These emerging markets offer the potential for businesses to generate additional revenue streams while reducing their environmental impact. Companies that are early adopters of these trends can gain a first-mover advantage and capture market share in rapidly expanding sectors.

d. Collaboration and Partnerships

Driving sustainable innovation often requires collaboration across industries, sectors, and regions. Businesses that embrace partnerships with governments, non-governmental organizations (NGOs), and other companies can leverage shared resources, knowledge, and expertise to accelerate their sustainability goals. For instance, companies working with NGOs or environmental organizations can gain access to critical data, research, and best practices that inform their sustainability strategies.

Cross-sector collaboration can also lead to the development of innovative solutions that address complex environmental challenges, such as reducing carbon emissions or developing sustainable infrastructure. By working together, companies can reduce the risks and costs associated with sustainable innovation while driving collective progress.

e. Regulatory Incentives and Government Support

As governments around the world increase their focus on sustainability, many are offering financial incentives, subsidies, or tax breaks to businesses that invest in sustainable innovation. These incentives can help offset the initial costs of adopting eco-friendly technologies, such as renewable energy or energy-efficient machinery.

Government support for sustainability initiatives often extends to research and development funding, enabling businesses to innovate without bearing

CHAPTER SEVEN

BUILDING AGILE TEAMS TO SUPPORT SCALABE MODEL

Building agile teams is essential for companies aiming to develop scalable models. Agility, in this context, refers to the ability of teams to adapt quickly to changes, efficiently manage complex projects, and remain resilient as the organization grows. Scaling a business requires more than just expanding operations, it demands flexible teams that can respond to market dynamics, customer needs, and technological advancements. To achieve this, companies must prioritize creating agile teams that support growth while maintaining productivity and innovation.

Fostering a Culture of Adaptability and Continuous Learning

In the fast-changing world of business, adaptability and continuous learning are critical for sustaining growth and innovation. A culture that encourages these traits enables organizations to navigate uncertainty, respond to market shifts, and remain competitive. It requires more than just offering training programs—it involves cultivating an environment where flexibility, curiosity, and a willingness to experiment are ingrained into the company's core values. By fostering this culture, businesses empower their teams to not only meet present challenges but also proactively prepare for the future.

i. Encouraging a Growth Mindset

The foundation of adaptability and continuous learning is a growth mindset—the belief that abilities and intelligence can be developed through dedication and hard work. Organizations that promote a growth mindset create a safe space for employees to take risks, experiment with new ideas, and learn from their mistakes without fear of judgment. Encouraging employees to view challenges as opportunities for learning fosters resilience and motivates them to seek out new skills and knowledge.

Leadership plays a vital role in modeling this mindset. By sharing their own learning experiences, failures, and growth, leaders can inspire their teams to adopt a similar approach. Regular feedback, both positive and constructive, is also essential in reinforcing the value of continuous improvement and the belief that learning is a lifelong journey.

ii. Building Learning and Development Programs

To support a culture of continuous learning, businesses must invest in structured learning and development programs. These programs can range from formal training sessions and workshops to more informal peer-to-peer learning and mentorship opportunities. Offering employees access to diverse learning resources—such as online courses, industry conferences, or internal knowledge-sharing platforms—gives them the tools to expand their expertise.

Additionally, businesses can encourage team members to take ownership of their learning by setting personal development goals aligned with both their career aspirations and the company's strategic objectives. Regularly revisiting these goals during performance reviews or one-on-one meetings ensures that continuous learning remains a priority throughout an employee's journey in the organization.

iii. Promoting Collaboration and Knowledge Sharing

Adaptability thrives in an environment where collaboration and open communication are encouraged. When employees from different teams and departments share knowledge, they bring unique perspectives and expertise that can drive innovation and problem-solving. Organizations can promote collaboration by breaking down silos, encouraging cross-functional teams, and creating spaces (physical or virtual) where employees can connect and exchange ideas.

One of the most effective ways to build a knowledge-sharing culture is through mentoring programs or "lunch and learn" sessions, where team members can learn from each other's experiences. Additionally, fostering a spirit of teamwork and open dialogue helps build trust within teams, allowing them to adapt more quickly to changes and leverage their collective skills.

iv. Leveraging Technology for Continuous Learning

Technology can significantly enhance the ability to foster a culture of adaptability and learning. Digital tools, such as learning management systems (LMS), allow employees to access educational content and track their progress, making learning more accessible and personalized. Companies can integrate gamification elements into their learning platforms to make skill development more engaging and motivating.

Further, analytics tools can help identify skill gaps within the organization, enabling leaders to tailor learning programs to specific needs. By using data to monitor progress and impact, companies can ensure that learning initiatives are aligned with business goals, making continuous improvement a measurable and strategic endeavor.

v. Recognizing and Rewarding Adaptability

Recognition and rewards are powerful motivators in cultivating adaptability. When employees are acknowledged for their ability to learn new skills, embrace change, or solve problems creatively, it reinforces the behaviors the organization wants to promote. Recognition can take many forms, from formal awards to simple expressions of appreciation in team meetings.

Additionally, creating incentives for employees who take on new challenges or acquire new skills can further encourage continuous development. Whether through promotions, additional responsibilities, or skill-based bonuses, companies that reward adaptability and learning demonstrate that these traits are valued and essential for growth.

Fostering a culture of adaptability and continuous learning positions businesses to thrive in ever-evolving markets. By promoting a growth mindset, investing in learning and development, encouraging collaboration, leveraging technology, and recognizing adaptability, companies can build teams that are prepared to handle future challenges. This culture not only helps employees develop personally and professionally but also ensures that the organization as a whole remains resilient and innovative in the face of change.

Implementing Cross-Functional Collaboration for Greater Efficiency

Cross-functional collaboration is a strategic approach to harness the diverse skills and expertise of various departments within an organization. By fostering open communication, breaking down silos, and encouraging shared goals, companies can significantly improve efficiency. Teams from different functional areas—such as marketing, operations, and technology—bring unique perspectives that, when aligned, lead to innovative solutions and streamlined processes.

Implementing this collaboration requires leadership commitment, clear objectives, and tools that facilitate real-time communication and project management. The result is not only faster decision-making but also a more agile organization, capable of adapting quickly to market changes and delivering superior results.

Empowering Teams with Tools and Technology for Agility

Equipping teams with the right tools and technologies is essential to fostering agility and supporting scalable business models. Agile teams rely on real-time communication, project management software, and data analytics tools to streamline workflows and make informed decisions. For example, project management platforms like Jira, Asana, or Trello allow teams to track tasks, set priorities, and collaborate seamlessly, while communication tools such as Slack enable rapid information sharing.

Additionally, adopting data-driven decision-making tools helps agile teams identify trends, predict customer behavior, and measure the success of new initiatives. These technologies enhance responsiveness and ensure that as a business scales, teams are not overwhelmed by increased workloads or complexity. Empowering teams with advanced tools allows them to maintain productivity and adaptability, even as the organization expands.

Building agile teams is key to supporting scalable models. By fostering a culture of adaptability, encouraging cross-functional collaboration, and equipping teams with the right tools, businesses can develop the agility needed to navigate growth while maintaining efficiency and innovation. Agile teams not only support the operational needs of a scaling company but also position the organization to respond proactively to future challenges and opportunities.

CHAPTER EIGHT

TECHNOLOGY INTEGRATION FOR OPERATIONAL EFFICIENCY

In today's fast-paced business environment, organizations are increasingly turning to technology integration as a means to enhance operational efficiency. By merging advanced digital tools and systems into everyday processes, companies can optimize workflows, improve productivity, and drive growth.

Automation of Routine Tasks

Automation of routine tasks has become a cornerstone of modern business operations, drastically reducing the need for manual intervention and enhancing overall efficiency. By implementing automation technologies, organizations can streamline repetitive processes that previously required significant time and human effort. This shift allows employees to focus on more strategic, value-driven activities, ultimately boosting productivity and innovation.

Tasks such as data entry, payroll processing, invoicing, and customer support can be automated using tools like Robotic Process Automation (RPA) and AI-driven software. These systems can perform tasks with a high degree of accuracy, minimizing the risk of human error and ensuring consistency. For instance, automated invoicing systems can handle thousands of transactions daily, reducing processing time from hours to minutes and improving cash flow management.

Automation also improves operational speed. In industries like manufacturing, automated machines can perform complex tasks far faster than manual labor, leading to shorter production cycles and increased output. In service industries, chatbots and virtual assistants can handle routine customer inquiries, offering instant responses and freeing up human agents for more complex issues.

Additionally, automation enhances scalability. As businesses grow, automated systems can handle increased volumes of work without the need for proportional increases in labor costs. This makes it easier for companies to expand their operations without being bogged down by inefficiencies.

While automation offers clear benefits, it also requires thoughtful implementation. Organizations must assess which tasks are best suited for automation and invest in the right technologies that integrate seamlessly with existing systems. Training and upskilling employees to work alongside these automated systems is also crucial, ensuring that human talent is fully leveraged in areas where creativity and problem-solving are essential.

Automating routine tasks not only minimizes manual efforts but also leads to significant time and cost savings, improved accuracy, and enhanced operational efficiency. It allows businesses to optimize their resources and remain competitive in an increasingly automated world.

Integrating Real-Time Data for Smarter Decision-Making

Integrating real-time data into business operations has become a vital strategy for making smarter, faster, and more informed decisions. As companies operate in an increasingly data-driven environment, having access to up-to-the-minute information is essential for maintaining a competitive edge. Real-time data integration allows organizations to monitor performance, respond quickly to market changes, and make data-backed decisions that drive success.

One of the key benefits of real-time data is its ability to provide instant insights. Instead of relying on static reports that may be outdated by the time they're reviewed, real-time data platforms allow decision-makers to access the most current information. For example, businesses can track customer behavior, sales trends, and inventory levels in real-time, enabling swift adjustments to marketing campaigns, pricing strategies, or supply chain management. This agility is crucial in fast-paced industries where market conditions can shift rapidly.

Real-time data also plays a pivotal role in operational efficiency. In industries such as manufacturing, transportation, and logistics, having access to real-time data from sensors and IoT devices enables companies to optimize processes on the fly. For example, monitoring equipment performance in real-time can help predict maintenance needs before breakdowns occur, minimizing downtime and reducing repair costs. Similarly, real-time data in logistics can help reroute deliveries based on traffic conditions or other disruptions, ensuring timely deliveries and improving customer satisfaction.

Another major advantage of real-time data integration is improved decision-making through enhanced analytics. By feeding real-time data into advanced analytics tools, businesses can apply machine learning algorithms and predictive models to forecast future trends and outcomes. This not only helps in identifying opportunities but also in mitigating risks. For instance, real-time financial data can help a company monitor cash flow closely and take immediate action to address shortfalls, while real-time marketing data can highlight campaigns that aren't performing well, enabling quick adjustments.

However, successful real-time data integration requires the right infrastructure and tools. Organizations must invest in systems that can capture, process, and visualize data in real-time, such as cloud-based data platforms, AI-powered analytics tools, and business intelligence dashboards. These systems need to be integrated seamlessly across departments, ensuring that data flows smoothly and is accessible to the people who need it most. Additionally, data security and privacy must be prioritized, as real-time data often includes sensitive information that must be protected from breaches or unauthorized access.

Training and empowering employees to leverage real-time data effectively is another crucial factor. Data should be presented in a user-friendly format that allows team members to interpret and act on the information without requiring deep technical expertise. When decision-makers across all levels of the organization have the right tools and knowledge, they can make faster, more accurate decisions that improve outcomes.

Integrating real-time data into business processes is a transformative step toward smarter decision-making. It enables companies to respond quickly to changing conditions, optimize operations, and make data-driven decisions that enhance efficiency and drive growth. By investing in the right technology and fostering a data-driven culture, businesses can unlock the full potential of real-time data and stay ahead of the competition.

Enhanced Collaboration Through Unified Communication Systems

Enhanced collaboration through unified communication systems has revolutionized the way teams work together, especially in an increasingly remote and distributed work environment. Unified communication systems integrate various communication tools such as messaging, video conferencing, voice calls, file sharing, and collaboration platforms into a single interface, creating a seamless flow of information across an organization. This integration eliminates the need to switch between different tools, improving collaboration, efficiency, and productivity.

One of the key advantages of unified communication systems is the ability to facilitate real-time collaboration. With tools like video conferencing, instant messaging, and shared workspaces, teams can communicate instantly regardless of location, breaking down geographical barriers. For instance, a marketing team in New York can seamlessly collaborate with a design team in London and a development team in Singapore, all within the same platform. Real-time collaboration speeds up decision-making and project execution, as teams can discuss, share ideas, and solve problems in the moment rather than relying on delayed communication methods like email.

Unified communication systems also improve coordination between departments. Many organizations struggle with departmental silos, where teams operate in isolation with little interaction or information sharing. A unified communication platform can help bridge these silos by enabling cross-functional teams to collaborate more effectively. For example, a sales team can easily share customer feedback with the product development team or loop in the customer support team on a product issue. This interconnectedness leads to better alignment of goals, quicker issue resolution, and a more cohesive organizational culture.

Additionally, unified communication systems enhance productivity by simplifying workflows. Instead of toggling between multiple apps email for communication, a separate platform for file sharing, and another for project management, employees can access everything they need in one place. This consolidation reduces the time spent on switching tasks and searching for information, allowing teams to focus more on their core responsibilities. Features such as shared calendars, integrated project management tools, and collaborative document editing further streamline work, ensuring that everyone stays aligned and on track with deadlines.

These systems also provide scalability and flexibility, which are crucial for growing businesses. As organizations expand, especially across multiple locations or with remote teams, a unified communication system can scale to accommodate new users and features without compromising performance. It allows businesses to adapt to changing communication needs, such as adding new channels or integrating third-party tools, without disrupting existing workflows. This flexibility ensures that as the organization grows, its communication infrastructure can keep pace.

Unified communication systems also contribute to better employee engagement and work satisfaction. In the modern workplace, employees value flexibility and seamless communication. With features like mobile access and cloud-based solutions, team members can stay connected and collaborate from anywhere, whether in the office, at home, or on the go. This accessibility not only supports remote work but also improves work-life balance, as employees can communicate more efficiently without the need for long commutes or extended hours in the office.

Despite the many benefits, implementing unified communication systems requires careful planning and execution. Organizations must select systems that align with their specific needs, ensuring that the platform supports both internal and external communication. Security and data protection are also critical considerations, as sensitive business information may be shared across the platform. Companies should adopt strong encryption, secure access protocols, and regular software updates to safeguard data.

Unified communication systems offer a powerful solution for enhancing collaboration in modern organizations. By integrating multiple communication tools into a single platform, these systems promote real-time collaboration, break down silos, and streamline workflows, leading to increased efficiency and productivity. As businesses continue to embrace remote work and digital transformation, unified communication platforms will play an essential role in fostering collaboration, driving innovation, and ensuring long-term success.

Enhanced Data Management and Analytics

Enhanced data management and analytics have become essential pillars for organizations seeking to gain a competitive advantage and drive operational efficiency. As businesses generate massive amounts of data from various sources, customer interactions, supply chains, sales transactions, and more effectively managing and analyzing this data is crucial for informed decision-making. Enhanced data management systems, combined with advanced analytics tools, allow organizations to turn raw data into actionable insights that can drive growth, innovation, and efficiency across all aspects of the business.

Importance of Enhanced Data Management

Effective data management begins with the organization's ability to collect, store, and access data in a systematic and secure manner. Without an efficient data management system, businesses risk data fragmentation, where critical information is scattered across various platforms or departments, making it difficult to retrieve and use.

i. Centralized Data Repositories: One of the primary features of enhanced data management is the creation of centralized data repositories. These can take the form of cloud-based storage solutions or on-premise databases where all organizational data is stored and managed in a single location. Centralizing data ensures that teams across the organization have access to the same up-to-date information, breaking down silos and promoting better collaboration.

ii. Data Governance: Effective data management also involves establishing data governance policies that ensure data quality, consistency, and security. This includes defining who has access to which data, how data is classified, and what measures are in place to protect sensitive information. Strong data governance ensures compliance with industry regulations such as GDPR or HIPAA and reduces the risk of data breaches or misuse.

iii. Data Integration: With enhanced data management, organizations can also integrate data from multiple sources. For example, customer data from CRM systems, transactional data from financial software, and operational data from supply chain management tools can all be combined into a single platform. Data integration helps create a comprehensive view of the business, enabling better decision-making and analysis.

Benefits of Enhanced Data Management and Analytics

Enhanced data management and analytics offer numerous benefits that can significantly impact an organization's performance and decision-making processes.

i. Improved Decision-Making: Perhaps the most significant benefit is improved decision-making. By having access to real-time, accurate data, and powerful analytics tools, decision-makers can base their strategies on facts and insights rather than intuition or guesswork. This leads to more effective resource allocation, better customer targeting, and smarter business investments.

ii. Operational Efficiency: Enhanced data management streamlines operations by providing a clear view of all processes within the organization. This allows businesses to identify inefficiencies, eliminate bottlenecks, and optimize workflows. For example, manufacturers can use data analytics to monitor equipment performance in real-time, predicting maintenance needs and preventing costly downtime.

iii. Customer Insights and Personalization: Businesses can gain deeper insights into customer behavior by analyzing data from multiple touchpoints, such as website interactions, purchase history, and social media engagement. This enables companies to personalize marketing efforts, improve customer experiences, and build stronger relationships. For example, e-commerce platforms can use data analytics to recommend products to customers based on their past browsing and purchase behavior, leading to increased sales and customer loyalty.

iv. Risk Mitigation: Advanced analytics can also help organizations identify and mitigate risks before they become critical. For instance, financial institutions use predictive analytics to detect potential fraudulent transactions in real-time. Similarly, supply chain managers can use data analytics to anticipate disruptions and adjust their operations accordingly, minimizing the impact of external factors such as delays or shortages.

Challenges of Enhanced Data Management and Analytics

Despite the significant advantages, implementing enhanced data management and analytics comes with challenges that organizations must address.

i. Data Quality Issues: Poor data quality can undermine even the most sophisticated analytics tools. If data is inaccurate, incomplete, or outdated, the insights generated will be unreliable. Organizations must invest in data cleansing and validation processes to ensure that their data is accurate and consistent across all sources.

ii. Integration Complexities: Integrating data from multiple sources can be complex, particularly when different departments use incompatible systems. Successful integration requires investment in data integration tools and platforms that can bridge these gaps, as well as collaboration between IT and business teams to ensure smooth implementation.

iii. Data Privacy and Security: With enhanced data management comes the responsibility to protect sensitive information. Organizations must adopt robust cybersecurity measures to safeguard data against breaches and comply with privacy regulations. Failure to secure data can lead to legal consequences and damage to a company's reputation.

iv. Skill Gaps: Leveraging advanced analytics requires skilled professionals who understand data science, AI, and machine learning. Many organizations face a shortage of talent in these areas, making it essential to invest in training and recruitment to build the necessary expertise.

Best Practices for Implementation

To maximize the benefits of enhanced data management and analytics, organizations should follow several best practices:

i. Develop a Data Strategy: A comprehensive data strategy should outline how the organization will collect, manage, and use data to achieve its business goals. This strategy should include data governance policies, privacy protocols, and a clear plan for integrating data across departments.

ii. Invest in the Right Technology: The right tools are crucial for success. Organizations should invest in scalable data management platforms, advanced analytics software, and cloud infrastructure that supports the seamless integration and processing of large volumes of data.

iii. Foster a Data-Driven Culture: Organizations should encourage a culture where data is valued and leveraged in decision-making at all levels. This involves training employees on how to use data and analytics tools and promoting collaboration between business and technical teams.

iv. Continuously Monitor and Improve: Data management and analytics should be treated as ongoing processes that require regular monitoring and improvement. Organizations should evaluate the performance of their systems, gather feedback, and make adjustments to ensure they continue to meet business needs.

Enhanced data management and analytics are critical for organizations seeking to thrive in a data-driven world. By effectively managing data and leveraging advanced analytics, businesses can gain deeper insights, improve decision-making, optimize operations, and stay ahead of the competition. While challenges exist, with the right strategies, technology, and culture, organizations can unlock the full potential of their data and drive sustainable growth and success.

Cloud and SaaS Solutions for Operational Flexibility

Cloud and Software-as-a-Service (SaaS) solutions have transformed the way businesses operate by offering unparalleled flexibility, scalability, and cost-effectiveness. These technologies allow companies to streamline their operations, reduce overhead costs, and respond swiftly to changes in the business environment. In an increasingly digital world, embracing cloud and SaaS solutions is no longer a luxury—it's a necessity for organizations that aim to stay competitive and agile.

Understanding Cloud Solutions

Cloud computing refers to the delivery of computing services—such as storage, databases, networking, software, and analytics—over the internet (the "cloud"). Instead of maintaining physical data centers and servers, businesses can access these resources on-demand from cloud providers like Amazon Web Services (AWS), Microsoft Azure, or Google Cloud. This eliminates the need for substantial upfront investments in hardware and IT infrastructure.

Cloud solutions are typically categorized into three types:

i. Infrastructure as a Service (IaaS): Provides virtualized computing resources over the internet. Businesses can rent virtual machines, storage, and networks on a pay-as-you-go basis.

ii. Platform as a Service (PaaS): Allows businesses to develop, run, and manage applications without the complexity of building and maintaining the underlying infrastructure.

iv. Software as a Service (SaaS): Delivers software applications over the internet, typically on a subscription basis. Users can access the software through a web browser without having to install or maintain it locally.

Operational Flexibility Through Cloud Solutions

One of the key advantages of cloud solutions is the flexibility they offer. Businesses can scale their resources up or down based on their needs, ensuring that they are not over-committing to hardware and resources. This flexibility translates into several operational benefits:

i. Scalability: Cloud services allow businesses to scale their IT resources on demand. For example, during peak seasons, an e-commerce platform can increase its computing power to handle a surge in traffic without investing in additional servers. Similarly, if demand decreases, the business can scale down, saving on operational costs. This flexibility is particularly beneficial for startups and small businesses that may experience rapid growth but lack the capital to invest in a large-scale infrastructure.

ii. Remote Accessibility: Cloud-based platforms enable employees to access applications and data from anywhere with an internet connection. This remote accessibility is crucial in today's workforce, where remote work and global teams are becoming more prevalent. Employees can collaborate on projects in real time, access critical business data, and continue their work seamlessly, whether they are at the office, at home, or on the go.

iii. Disaster Recovery and Business Continuity: Cloud solutions offer robust disaster recovery capabilities. In traditional IT environments, recovering from data loss or system failures often involves complex and expensive processes. With cloud solutions, data is continuously backed up in multiple locations, ensuring that businesses can quickly recover from disruptions. This ensures continuity of operations, minimizing downtime and potential revenue loss.

iv. Cost Efficiency: By leveraging cloud services, businesses can reduce their capital expenditures on physical hardware, servers, and data centers. Instead, they can shift to a more flexible operational expenditure model, paying only for the resources they use. This "pay-as-you-go" model eliminates the need for costly IT maintenance, upgrades, and staffing, allowing organizations to allocate their resources to other critical business areas.

SaaS Solutions for Enhanced Flexibility

SaaS platforms offer even greater operational flexibility by providing software applications over the internet without the need for installation, management, or updates. Businesses can subscribe to a variety of SaaS solutions that cater to different operational needs, such as customer relationship management

(CRM), human resources (HR), project management, accounting, and more. These platforms can be customized and integrated seamlessly with existing systems, improving efficiency and collaboration.

Some of the key benefits of SaaS solutions include:

i. Easy Deployment and Updates: SaaS applications are typically ready to use right after subscription. This reduces the time needed for installation, setup, and customization. Additionally, software updates and patches are automatically managed by the service provider, ensuring that businesses always have access to the latest features and security updates without any downtime or additional effort from IT teams.

ii. Collaboration and Mobility: SaaS solutions promote collaboration by allowing multiple users to access the same platform and work on shared files or projects in real time. For example, SaaS-based project management tools like Asana or Trello enable teams to track project progress, assign tasks, and share documents from anywhere in the world. Similarly, Google Workspace allows employees to collaborate on documents, spreadsheets, and presentations simultaneously, enhancing productivity and teamwork.

iii. Subscription-Based Pricing: SaaS solutions typically operate on a subscription-based pricing model, which provides businesses with predictable, recurring expenses. This model is cost-effective, particularly for small and medium-sized enterprises (SMEs) that might not have the resources to invest in expensive software licenses. Subscriptions can often be scaled up or down depending on the number of users, allowing businesses to manage costs efficiently.

iv. Customization and Integration: Modern SaaS platforms are highly customizable, allowing businesses to tailor the software to their specific needs. Many SaaS applications also integrate with other software and systems, such as accounting tools, CRM systems, or enterprise resource planning (ERP) platforms. This integration simplifies workflows, reduces redundancies, and ensures that all business processes are aligned.

The Role of Cloud and SaaS in Digital Transformation

As companies continue to embrace digital transformation, cloud and SaaS solutions play a pivotal role in helping organizations become more agile and responsive to market demands. These technologies allow businesses to quickly adopt new tools, enter new markets, and innovate without the limitations of traditional IT infrastructure.

i. Agility in Product Development: Cloud-based development platforms allow businesses to build, test, and deploy applications faster than ever before. With PaaS solutions, development teams can work in agile environments, rapidly iterating on product features and deploying updates seamlessly. This agility shortens time-to-market and enables businesses to respond quickly to customer feedback or market changes.

ii. Data-Driven Decision-Making: SaaS solutions often come with built-in analytics and reporting capabilities that provide real-time insights into business performance. Cloud-based data platforms allow businesses to collect and analyze large volumes of data without the need for extensive infrastructure investments. With cloud-based AI and machine learning tools, companies can analyze customer behavior, predict trends, and make data-driven decisions that enhance operational efficiency.

iii. Enhanced Customer Experience: By leveraging cloud and SaaS solutions, businesses can deliver better customer experiences. Cloud-based CRM systems like Salesforce or HubSpot allow companies to manage customer interactions across multiple channels, providing personalized service and support. With SaaS tools, businesses can easily scale their customer service teams, implement automated chatbots, and provide self-service portals, ensuring customers receive timely and efficient support.

Challenges and Considerations

Despite the many benefits of cloud and SaaS solutions, businesses must also address certain challenges and considerations:

i. Data Security and Privacy: As businesses move their data to the cloud, they must ensure that strong security measures are in place. Cloud providers typically offer robust security protocols, but businesses must still implement additional safeguards, such as encryption, access controls, and regular audits, to protect sensitive data. Compliance with data protection regulations such as GDPR is also essential when using cloud-based services.

ii. Vendor Lock-In: Relying heavily on a specific cloud or SaaS provider can lead to vendor lock-in, making it difficult to switch providers or move data to another platform in the future. Businesses should carefully evaluate service agreements and consider multi-cloud strategies or hybrid cloud solutions to mitigate the risk of vendor lock-in.

iii. Integration with Legacy Systems: Many businesses still rely on legacy systems that may not be fully compatible with cloud or SaaS platforms. Integrating these systems can be complex and may require significant investment in custom development or middleware. However, the long-term benefits of increased flexibility and scalability often outweigh the initial challenges of integration.

Best Practices for Implementing Cloud and SaaS Solutions

To successfully implement cloud and SaaS solutions and maximize their benefits, businesses should consider the following best practices:

i. Assess Business Needs: Before adopting cloud or SaaS solutions, businesses should conduct a thorough assessment of their operational needs, existing infrastructure, and goals. This ensures that the chosen solutions align with the company's strategic objectives and provide tangible value.

ii. Choose the Right Providers: Selecting the right cloud or SaaS provider is critical. Businesses should evaluate providers based on factors such as security, scalability, pricing, and customer support. It's also important to choose vendors that offer flexible contract terms and reliable service level agreements (SLAs).

iii. Plan for Integration: Successful implementation of cloud and SaaS solutions requires seamless integration with existing systems. Businesses should work with experienced IT teams or consultants to develop an integration plan that minimizes disruption and ensures smooth data flow between platforms.

iv. Train Employees: To fully leverage the capabilities of cloud and SaaS platforms, businesses should provide training to employees. Ensuring that staff members are proficient in using these tools will enhance productivity and improve collaboration.

Cloud and SaaS solutions offer businesses unparalleled operational flexibility, scalability, and cost savings, making them essential tools for navigating the complexities of today's business environment. By leveraging these technologies, organizations can streamline their operations, enhance collaboration, improve customer experiences, and respond swiftly to market changes. However, to fully realize the benefits, businesses must carefully assess their needs, choose the right providers, and plan for seamless integration. In an era defined by digital transformation, cloud and SaaS solutions are crucial for driving growth, innovation, and long-term success.

Ensuring Cybersecurity and Data Integrity

Ensuring cybersecurity and data integrity has become a critical focus for organizations worldwide as cyber threats evolve in sophistication and volume. As businesses increasingly rely on digital systems to store, manage, and process vast amounts of data, protecting sensitive information and maintaining its accuracy are fundamental to safeguarding operations, reputation, and customer trust. A comprehensive approach to cybersecurity and data integrity involves deploying advanced technologies, fostering security-conscious cultures, and adhering to best practices for data governance.

The Importance of Cybersecurity in the Modern World

In today's hyper-connected digital landscape, the risk of cyberattacks has grown exponentially. Cybercriminals use a wide range of tactics, including phishing, ransomware, malware, and distributed denial-of-service (DDoS) attacks, to exploit vulnerabilities in organizational systems. These attacks can result in data breaches, financial loss, and significant damage to an organization's reputation. The rise in remote work, cloud computing, and the Internet of Things (IoT) has expanded the attack surface for businesses, making cybersecurity a top priority.

i. Data Breaches and Financial Impact: Data breaches expose sensitive information such as customer data, intellectual property, and financial records. According to studies, the average cost of a data breach can run into millions of dollars, depending on the scale of the incident and the industry. In addition to the direct financial losses, companies may face legal liabilities, regulatory fines, and lost business opportunities as a result of eroded customer trust.

ii. Reputation and Trust: In the digital economy, trust is a key driver of business success. Organizations that fail to secure customer data or suffer from repeated security incidents risk long-term damage to their brand. Customers and partners expect their data to be handled securely, and any failure in this regard can lead to a loss of credibility, market share, and customer loyalty.

Key Elements of Cybersecurity

To ensure cybersecurity, businesses must adopt a multi-layered approach, combining technical defenses with policies, employee training, and continuous monitoring.

i. Access Control and Identity Management: One of the first lines of defense in cybersecurity is ensuring that only authorized users have access to systems and data. This requires robust identity management protocols, including multi-factor authentication (MFA), role-based access controls (RBAC), and secure password policies. MFA adds an extra layer of security by requiring users to provide two or more verification factors before accessing a system. RBAC limits access to information based on an individual's role within the organization, ensuring that employees only have access to the data necessary for their job functions.

ii. Network Security: Securing the organization's network infrastructure is critical for preventing unauthorized access and attacks. Firewalls, intrusion detection systems (IDS), and intrusion prevention systems (IPS) are essential tools for monitoring and controlling network traffic. Encryption protocols ensure that sensitive data transmitted over networks is protected from eavesdropping or tampering. Virtual private networks (VPNs) are commonly used to secure connections between remote employees and the organization's internal systems, especially in environments where remote work is prevalent.

iii. Endpoint Security: With the increasing use of personal devices for work, endpoint security has become a crucial component of cybersecurity. This includes deploying antivirus software, patch management systems, and endpoint detection and response (EDR) tools to protect individual devices (laptops, smartphones, tablets) from malware, ransomware, and other forms of attack. Organizations must ensure that all devices connected to their network are updated with the latest security patches and configurations.

iv. Encryption: Data encryption ensures that information remains secure both at rest (stored on devices or servers) and in transit (during communication or data transfer). By converting sensitive data into an unreadable format, encryption prevents unauthorized individuals from accessing it, even if they manage to intercept the data. End-to-end encryption is especially important for securing communications such as emails and instant messaging.

v. Incident Response and Recovery: No security system is foolproof, and organizations must be prepared to respond quickly and effectively to cyber incidents. An incident response plan outlines the steps the organization will take to contain and mitigate an attack, minimize damage, and restore normal operations. Regular incident response drills, along with clearly defined roles and communication channels, are essential for ensuring that teams are ready to respond under pressure.

Data Integrity and Its Importance

While cybersecurity focuses on protecting data from unauthorized access and breaches, data integrity is concerned with maintaining the accuracy, consistency, and reliability of data throughout its lifecycle. Data integrity ensures that information is not altered or corrupted, either accidentally or maliciously, and that it remains trustworthy for decision-making and compliance purposes.

i. Accuracy and Consistency: Data integrity guarantees that the information used by an organization is accurate and reflects real-world conditions. Inaccurate or inconsistent data can lead to flawed decision-making, financial losses, and reputational harm. For example, if financial records or customer information are corrupted, it can result in errors in financial reporting, invoicing, or customer service interactions.

ii. Compliance and Regulatory Requirements: Many industries are subject to stringent regulations regarding data accuracy, particularly in sectors such as healthcare, finance, and government. Organizations must ensure that their data remains intact to comply with standards such as the Health Insurance Portability and Accountability Act (HIPAA), the General Data Protection Regulation (GDPR), and Sarbanes-Oxley (SOX). Failure to maintain data integrity can result in significant fines and legal consequences.

iii. Protection from Malicious Tampering: In addition to accidental errors, data integrity must be protected from malicious tampering. Cybercriminals may seek to manipulate or corrupt data as part of a broader attack, such as altering financial records to conceal fraud or disrupting critical infrastructure systems. Ensuring data integrity involves implementing safeguards that detect and prevent unauthorized changes, as well as mechanisms for restoring data to its original state if tampering occurs.

Strategies for Ensuring Data Integrity

To maintain data integrity, organizations must implement a range of technical and procedural measures designed to ensure that data remains accurate, consistent, and secure over time.

i. Data Validation and Verification: Data validation ensures that the information entered into a system meets predefined criteria for accuracy and completeness. This is especially important during data entry processes, where human error can introduce inconsistencies. Verification involves cross-checking data against known sources to ensure its correctness.

ii. Audit Trails and Logging: Maintaining detailed audit trails is essential for tracking changes to data and identifying when and by whom data was altered. Audit trails provide a historical record of data modifications, making it easier to detect unauthorized changes or errors. Logging systems also help organizations monitor access to sensitive data and can be used to identify suspicious behavior or patterns indicative of insider threats.

iii. Backup and Recovery Solutions: Regular backups are a critical component of both cybersecurity and data integrity strategies. In the event of data corruption, loss, or a ransomware attack, having reliable backups allows an organization to quickly restore data to its original state. Backup strategies should follow the 3-2-1 rule: maintaining three copies of data, on two different media types, with one copy stored offsite.

iv. Data Encryption and Digital Signatures: Encryption not only protects data from unauthorized access but also plays a key role in ensuring its integrity. By encrypting data, organizations can ensure that any unauthorized modifications render the data unusable. Digital signatures further enhance integrity by providing a verifiable way to ensure that data has not been tampered with during transmission.

v. Data Loss Prevention (DLP) Systems: DLP solutions help organizations prevent the unauthorized sharing or exfiltration of sensitive data. By monitoring and controlling data flow within the organization, DLP systems can detect attempts to transfer data outside authorized channels and prevent accidental or malicious data leaks.

Human Factor and Security Awareness

One of the most significant vulnerabilities in both cybersecurity and data integrity strategies is the human factor. Employees, contractors, and third-party vendors all play a role in maintaining security, and their actions can either strengthen or weaken defenses.

i. Employee Training and Awareness: Regular cybersecurity awareness training helps employees recognize potential threats such as phishing emails, social engineering attacks, and unsafe online practices. Employees should be educated on the importance of strong passwords, the risks associated with public Wi-Fi, and how to securely handle sensitive data. Creating a security-conscious culture within the organization ensures that employees remain vigilant and proactive in maintaining data integrity.

ii. Insider Threats: Insider threats, whether intentional or accidental, pose a significant risk to both cybersecurity and data integrity. Employees or contractors with privileged access to sensitive systems and data can intentionally alter, delete, or exfiltrate information. To mitigate this risk, organizations should implement strong access controls, monitor privileged user activities, and enforce strict data governance policies.

Emerging Technologies in Cybersecurity and Data Integrity

As the threat landscape evolves, new technologies are emerging to help organizations enhance cybersecurity and protect data integrity.

i. Artificial Intelligence (AI) and Machine Learning: AI-powered cybersecurity tools can analyze vast amounts of data in real-time, detecting unusual patterns or behaviors that may indicate a cyberattack. Machine learning algorithms can help identify new and evolving threats that may not be detected by traditional signature-based defenses. AI also plays a role in automating incident response processes, allowing organizations to react more quickly to potential breaches.

ii. Blockchain for Data Integrity: Blockchain technology offers a new way to ensure data integrity by providing an immutable, decentralized ledger of transactions. Once data is recorded on the blockchain, it cannot be altered without consensus from the network, making it a powerful tool for preventing tampering and ensuring data accuracy. Blockchain is increasingly being explored for applications such as supply chain management, financial transactions, and healthcare records.

iii. Zero Trust Architecture: Zero trust security models assume that no user or system, whether inside or outside the organization, should be trusted by default. Instead, access to systems and data is continuously verified and authenticated. By adopting a zero trust approach, organizations can reduce the risk of unauthorized access and ensure that only verified users are allowed to interact with sensitive data.

Ensuring cybersecurity and data integrity is a complex, ongoing process that requires a combination of advanced technologies